SALADS

fresh, delicious dishes for all occasions

SALADS

fresh, delicious dishes for all occasions

STERLING
New York

contents

introduction

With the great variety of produce now available, it's no wonder salads have become the stars of modern cuisine. Salad is wonderfully versatile – it can be served as a starter, side dish, an impressive main meal, and a refreshing dessert. Salads offer a variety of textures, colors and flavors to a meal, and are an easy way to enjoy an abundance of fresh ingredients every day.

The popularity of salads is evident from the increasing number of salad bars and the availability of ready-to-use salad stuffs in supermarkets. And the greater availability of fresh and exotic ingredients has meant that our salads have become more interesting and enticing.

The leafy greens used for salads can range from iceberg, romaine, chicory, radicchio, endive, arugula, watercress to baby spinach leaves. It is essential to select well when you buy. The golden rule is to purchase in season, when they are at their peak and, therefore, less expensive. Thoroughly wash all your salad greens, whether they have been pre-washed or not. Dry well, preferably in a salad spinner, but a clean tea towel will also do the trick.

Color, flavor and crunch can be added with vegetables like bell peppers, corn, red onion and asparagus. Avocado, with its rich buttery flesh, is the perfect partner for a salad containing seafood, such as shrimp or salmon. Pecans, walnuts, almonds or pine nuts, toasted in a skillet, provide a delicious crunch when sprinkled on top of a salad, or try the Soy salad seed mix on the next page.

Salad tips

Storage

Store leafy salad greens in the crisper of your refrigerator in order to keep them fresh. Herbs should be kept standing upright in a glass half-filled with water and covered with a plastic bag. Alternatively line an airtight plastic container with a paper towel, lay the herbs on top, cover with another dry paper towel and seal the lid, then store in the fridge. Tomatoes and avocados should always be kept at room temperature until fully ripe, as they will not ripen after chilling.

Dressings

Dressings can vary from a simple vinaigrette to the rich and creamy. Different kinds of salads require different dressings – a simple vinaigrette is best on a complicated salad; a sharp vinegary dressing is good on tomato salads; a creamy dressing is lovely on crisp or soft salad leaves. For a different twist use lemon juice instead of vinegar or try avocado instead of mayo in creamy dressings.

How to dress a salad

Avoid overdressing salads as this can drown out the other flavors. Almost all of us make more dressing than we need. Just before serving, pour on about half as much dressing as you think you'll need and toss the salad. You can always add a little more if necessary. Season to taste with salt and pepper just before serving.

Cooking vegetables for salads

There are some vegetables that go particularly well in salads: snow peas, sugar snap peas, asparagus, broccolini, and beans. They should be blanched, or very lightly boiled, steamed or cooked in the microwave until still crisp – never ever mushy. Immediately drain your veggies and rinse in cold water to prevent any further cooking and to retain their bright color. Dry well before adding to your salad. Roasted vegetables make wonderful warm salads: sweet potato, pumpkin, potato and beets are delicious teamed with feta or goat cheese. Beets, either roasted or canned, should always be added at the last minute. Their rich beautiful color doesn't look so striking when is has bled through the salad and turned everything pink.

Salad seed mixtures

Looking for a tasty alternative to croutons? Try this easy-to-make see mix instead. Sprinkle them over salads or steamed or baked vegetables when you want a nutty crunch.

Soy salad seed mix

¼ cup sesame seeds
¼ cup sunflower seeds
¼ cup pepitas
2 tablespoons pine nuts
1 tablespoon soy sauce

Toast seeds and pine nuts in dry skillet over medium-high heat, taking care not to allow them to burn, stirring constantly until the sesame seeds start to pop and the rest of the ingredients toast slightly. Place immediately in a bowl then stir in soy sauce while seed mixture is hot. Store in an airtight container in the fridge.

oils

1 Olive oil

The juice extracted from fresh olives. Extra virgin olive oil is the oil extracted from the first cold pressing and contains the most health benefits. Extra virgin olive oil can range in flavor from mild and fruity to robust and peppery.

'Pure', 'light' and 'extra light' olive oils have been refined and they lack the aroma, flavor and the natural antioxidant content of extra virgin olive oil. In fact the word "light" refers only to their light color, aroma and flavor, not to fat content. All olive oils have the same fat content.

Price is usually a guide to quality. Buy olive oil in small quantities – it becomes rancid over time – and store in a cool, dark place.

2 Peanut oil

Pressed from ground peanuts. It is most commonly used in Asian cooking because of its high smoke point – the capacity to handle high heat without burning.

3 Vegetable oil

Any of a number of oils sourced from plant rather than animal fats; it is flavorless and odorless so ideal when you need a bland oil.

4 Sesame oil

Made from roasted, crushed, white sesame seeds. Has a very strong flavor and is used sparingly, more as a flavoring than a cooking medium.

5 Walnut oil, hazelnut oil, macadamia oil

All have a distinctive nutty flavor. They are used in dressings and sauces, and can add a lovely nutty quality to baking.

1 Balsamic vinegar

Very distinctive Italian vinegar; there are now many balsamic vinegars on the market, ranging in pungency and quality depending on how, and for how long, they have been aged. The rich, sweet, and complex flavor becomes more mellow and sweet with age. It is used in salad dressings and is especially good when teamed with the pepperiness of arugula.

Supermarket-quality balsamic has been used to develop the recipes in this book. If using aged imported vinegar, use smaller quantities than suggested. For example, use 1 teaspoon of excellent quality balsamic instead of 1 tablespoon of supermarket-quality balsamic.

2 White balsamic vinegar

Made from white wine vinegar; the flavor is almost identical to regular balsamic vinegar; recipes usually include it (instead of regular balsamic vinegar) for aesthetic reasons, so as not to color sauces or dressings.

3 Cider vinegar

Also known as apple cider vinegar; made from fermented apples and has a brownish-yellow color. It has a distinctive sweet apple flavor and goes particularly well in relishes, dressings and pork dishes.

4 White wine vinegar, red wine vinegar

Made respectively from white wine and red wine. As with wine, there is a considerable range in quality. Both are commonly used in salad dressings. Both give a more mellow rounded flavor than white or malt vinegar.

5 Malt vinegar

A classic condiment for fish and chips; it is traditionally made from unhopped beer and has a strong flavor that is good for robust-flavored dressings, pickles and relishes.

6 Rice vinegar, rice wine vinegar

Made from fermented rice and flavored with sugar and salt. Its delicate flavor makes it very versatile; it is used in the preparation of sushi rice, is lovely in salad dressings and is often used in Asian dipping sauces.

7 Sherry vinegar

Natural vinegar aged in oak according to the traditional Spanish system; a mellow wine vinegar, sweeter than red or white wine vinegar, and named for its color. It is beautiful in a vinaigrette and is excellent when used for deglazing roasting and skillets pans when making a sauce.

vinegars

mustards

1 English, hot english
Traditional hot, pungent, deep-yellow mustard. Serve with roast beef and ham; wonderful with hard cheeses.

2 Wholegrain, honey wholegrain
A coarse grain mustard made from crushed mustard seeds and Dijon-style French mustard. Works well with cold meats and sausages.

3 Dijon, honey dijon
French in origin, pale brown and creamy with a fairly mild flavor. Delicious in salad dressings, especially for potato salad, and on meat.

4 American
Bright yellow in color, a sweet mustard containing mustard seeds, sugar, salt, spices and garlic. Serve with hot dogs and hamburgers.

1 Flat-leaf parsley
Often referred to as 'italian' parley, it is stronger in flavor and darker in color than curly parsley.

2 Oregano
Particularly prominent in Italian and Greek cuisines, it is often used with grilled meat, in tomato sauce, soup and on pizzas.

3 Mint
Often used with lamb, potatoes, peas and in fruit salads, and the sprigs are used in drinks and to make a simple tea. There are many varieties available.

4 Vietnamese mint
Identified mainly with Vietnamese cuisine, it is stronger in flavor and more peppery than regular mint and is commonly used fresh in salads and in rice paper rolls.

5 Basil

Also known as sweet basil, it is particularly popular in Italian dishes and the main ingredient of pesto; used with tomatoes.

6 Thai basil

One of the identifying flavors of Thai food, it has a slight aniseed taste. The leaves are smaller than sweet basil and the stems are purple.

7 Cilantro

Used in a wide variety of cuisines, from Latin American to South-East Asian, the leaves of the corinder planet lend a distinct flavor; it has a pungent aroma and taste and is a must in Thai green curry. Dried coriander seeds cannot be used as a substitute.

8 Tarragon

An essential flavor in many classic French dishes, it has a strong aniseed flavor. Be sure to use the French variety, not Russian, as the Russian is not nearly as aromatic and flavorful as its French counterpart.

9 Chives

Related to the onion and leek, it has a subtle onion flavor and is often used with eggs, in salads or as a garnish.

10 Thyme, lemon thyme

A member of the mint family, the strong aromatic leaves are very versatile and are often used in soups, meat dishes, particularly terrines and pâtés, and are a lovely alternative to rosemary on roast potatoes. Lemon thyme has a strong citrus aroma and flavor.

11 Dill

The distinctly feathery, frond-like leaves have an aniseed/celery sweetness and are good with potato salad and fish.

12 Rosemary

Sprig of long, thin pointy leaves with a strong pungent flavor, it is particularly good on roast potatoes and with lamb.

13 Chervil

Mild fennel-flavored member of the parsley family; a staple in French cuisine and is often used in egg dishes, salads and soups.

herbs

1 Iceberg lettuce

Heavy, firm round lettuce with tightly packed leaves and crisp texture.

2 Romaine lettuce, baby romaine lettuce

Elongated in shape with leaves ranging from dark green on the outside to almost white near the core; the traditional caesar salad lettuce.

3 Butter lettuce

Round, loosely formed head with a sweet flavor and soft, pale green leaves.

4 Mesclun

Commercial blend of green salad leaves, including baby spinach leaves, mizuna and curly endive.

5 Oak leaf lettuce

Soft, curly-leafed lettuce found in both green and red varieties.

6 Arugula

A peppery green leaf eaten raw in salads or wilted in rice and pasta dishes. Baby arugula leaves are smaller and less peppery.

7 Radicchio

Italian in origin, this lettuce brings a deep purple color and a distinctive bitter flavor to salads. It can also be cooked, usually grilled or tossed through hot pasta until just wilted. It does lose its crimson color when heated, but will develop a sweet, mellow flavor.

8 Baby spinach leaves

Small, bright green leaves that are best eaten raw in salads or cooked until barely wilted.

9 Red coral lettuce

Very curly and tightly furled red leaves that resemble coral and have a mild, sweet taste.

10 Mizuna, baby mizuna

A Japanese green with serrated, dark green leaves with narrow white stalks and a mild peppery flavor; often found in mesclun. Baby mizuna are lighter and have a milder flavor. Mizuna is most commonly used fresh in salads or added to soups and stir-fries.

11 Tat soi, baby tat soi

A Chinese green with dark green spoon-shaped leaves and distinctive long, white stalks; has a soft creamy texture and a subtle flavor. Baby tat soi is smaller and lighter in color.

salad leaves

12 White witlof, red witlof, baby witlof

Witlof, meaning "white leaf" in Dutch; also known as belgian endive; narrow, elongated bulbous clusters of leaves that are creamy white to light yellow in color and slightly bitter in flavor; the whiter the leaf, the less bitter the taste. Red varieties are also available, as well as baby witlof which is slightly less bitter. All can be eaten fresh, either chopped in salads or whole, or cooked. The flavor mellows and becomes less bitter with cooking.

13 Frisée

Related to chicory, frisée has a fairly bitter flavor with narrow and prickly looking curly outer leaves and an edible white heart.

14 Savoy cabbage

Heavy round head with tightly packed light green, crinkly leaves. It has a mild, sweet flavor.

15 Red cabbage

Deep purple in color, the inner leaves are tightly packed while the outer leaves are softer and more loosely attached and resemble a flower. It is often braised, pickled or shredded and eaten raw in salads.

16 Watercress

Deep green, clover-shaped leaves that have a peppery, spicy flavor. It is most commonly used in salads or made into a delightful soup.

17 Lamb's lettuce

Also known as corn salad, it has round or spoon shaped velvety green leaves with a mild nutty flavor. It is usually used in salads but can also be cooked until just wilted.

18 Snow pea tendrils

The thin, delicately crisp new growth of the snow pea plant, including the tender uppermost leaves and the tendrils that enable the plant to climb. These delicious tendrils are full of pea flavor and are often used as a garnish. If you can't find them, use snow pea sprouts instead.

19 Snow pea sprouts

Thin, light-green shoots and leaves with a smooth white to light green stalk; they have a delicate, sweet flavor and can be eaten raw, used in soups, steamed, or stir-fried.

20 Bean sprouts

Tender new growths of assorted beans and seeds. The most readily available are mung bean, soybean and alfalfa sprouts. They are often used in salads, stir-fries or sandwiches.

classic salads

Chopped salad ingredients vary from recipe to recipe; the only common rule is that all the ingredients are 'chopped'. You can also place all of the roughly chopped ingredients on a large chopping board and use a large knife to chop them all together.

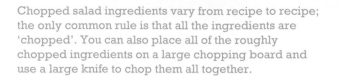

chopped salad

1 head romaine lettuce, coarsely chopped
1 raddicchio, coarsely chopped
1 large red bell pepper, coarsely chopped
1 small red onion, finely chopped
1 English cucumber, coarsely chopped
3 large tomatoes, coarsely chopped
2 celery stalks, trimmed, finely chopped
2 red radishes, sliced thinly
1 cup coarsely chopped fresh flat-leaf parsley
½ cup coarsely chopped fresh basil
4 ounces feta, crumbled
2 tablespoons red wine vinegar
2 tablespoons extra virgin olive oil

1 Place ingredients in large serving bowl; toss gently to combine.

prep time 15 minutes **serves** 4

caesar salad

½ loaf ciabatta (8 ounces)
1 clove garlic, crushed
⅓ cup olive oil
2 eggs
3 trimmed, leaves separated
  small heads romaine lettuce
1 cup grated Parmesan cheese caesar dressing
1 clove garlic, crushed
1 tablespoon Dijon mustard
2 tablespoons lemon juice
2 teaspoons Worcestershire sauce
2 tablespoons olive oil

1 Preheat oven to 350°F (325°F convection).

2 Cut bread into 1-inch cubes; combine garlic and oil in large bowl with bread. Arrange cubes on rimmed baking sheet and toast until croûtons are browned.

3 Place ingredients for caesar dressing in screw-top jar; shake well.

4 Bring water to the boil in small saucepan, add eggs; cover pan tightly, remove from heat. Remove eggs from water after 2 minutes. When cool enough to handle, break eggs into large bowl; add lettuce, mixing gently so egg coats leaves.

5 Add cheese, croutons and dressing to bowl; toss gently to combine.

prep & cook time 45 minutes **serves** 4

panzanella

4 cups water
½ loaf (8 ounces) stale sourdough bread,
  cut into 1-inch slices
2 large tomatoes, coarsely chopped
1 small red onion, thinly sliced
1 English cucumber, coarsely chopped
1 cup firmly packed fresh basil leaves
2 tablespoons olive oil
2 tablespoons red wine vinegar
1 clove garlic, crushed

1 Place the water in large shallow bowl; briefly dip bread slices into water. Pat dry with absorbent paper; tear bread into large chunks.

2 Place bread in large bowl with remaining ingredients; toss gently to combine.

prep time 20 minutes **serves** 4

caesar salad

panzanella

caprese salad

3 large roma tomatoes, thinly sliced
8 ounces fresh mozzarella, thinly sliced
2 tablespoons olive oil
¼ cup firmly packed fresh basil, torn

1 Overlap slices of tomato and cheese on serving platter.

2 Drizzle with oil; sprinkle with basil.

prep time 15 minutes **serves** 4

greek salad

4 roma tomatoes, thinly sliced
1 English cucumber, coarsely chopped
1 small red onion, thinly sliced
½ cup pitted kalamata olives
5 ounces crumbled feta
2 tablespoons olive oil
2 tablespoons lemon juice
2 teaspoons fresh oregano

1 Combine tomato, cucumber, onion, olives and feta in large bowl.

2 Place remaining ingredients in screw-top jar; shake well. Drizzle dressing over salad.

prep time 15 minutes **serves** 4

caprese salad

greek salad

salade niçoise

1 pound baby new potatoes, halved
½ pound baby green beans, trimmed
2 tablespoons olive oil
1 tablespoon lemon juice
2 tablespoons white wine vinegar
4 tomatoes, cut into wedges
4 hard-boiled eggs, quartered
1 (12-ounces) can tuna, drained, flaked
½ cup drained caperberries, rinsed
½ cup pitted small black olives
¼ cup firmly packed fresh flat-leaf parsley

1 Boil, steam or microwave potatoes and beans until tender; drain. Rinse under cold water; drain.

2 Whisk oil, juice, vinegar in large bowl; add potatoes, beans and remaining ingredients, mix gently.

prep & cook time 20 minutes   **serves** 4

chicken salad

4 cups boiling water
4 cups chicken stock
3 boneless, skinless chicken breasts (8 ounces each)
1 loaf French bread (12-ounces), thinly sliced
2 tablespoons olive oil
½ cup mayonnaise
½ cup sour cream
2 tablespoons lemon juice
4 stalks celery, trimmed, thinly sliced
1 white onion, finely chopped
3 large dill pickles, thinly sliced
2 tablespoons finely chopped fresh flat-leaf parsley
1 tablespoon finely chopped fresh tarragon
1 large head butter lettuce, leaves separated

1 Bring the water and stock to a gentle boil in large skillet; poach chicken, covered, about 10 minutes or until cooked through. Cool chicken in liquid 10 minutes; slice thinly. Discard liquid.

2 Meanwhile, preheat broiler. Brush both sides of bread slices with oil and arrange on baking sheet. Broil 1-2 minutes per side until lightly browned.

3 Whisk mayonnaise, cream and juice in small bowl.

4 Place chicken in large bowl with celery, onion, pickle and herbs; toss gently to combine.

5 Place lettuce leaves on serving platter; top with salad and bread, drizzle with mayonnaise mixture.

prep & cook time 50 minutes   **serves** 4

salade niçoise

chicken salad

waldorf salad

4 red apples
1 cup coarsely chopped walnuts
¼ cup lemon juice
5 stalks celery, trimmed, coarsely chopped
1 cup mayonnaise

1 Core unpeeled apples; cut into thin wedges.

2 Toast walnuts in a dry skillet over medium-high heat until fragrant.

3 Place apple in large serving bowl with remaining ingredients; toss gently to combine.

prep time 15 minutes   **serves** 4

lemon-garlic
spicy potato salad

1½ pounds baby new potatoes, unpeeled,
  cut into 1½-inch slices
½ cup coarsely chopped fresh flat-leaf parsley
¼ cup coarsely chopped fresh chives

lemon-garlic butter
8 tablespoons (1 stick) butter, softened
2 cloves garlic, crushed
1 tablespoon fresh lemon zest
1 teaspoon crushed red pepper flakes

1 Combine ingredients for lemon and chili butter in small bowl.

2 Boil, steam or microwave potato until tender; drain.

3 Combine hot potato, lemon-garlic butter, parsley and chives in large bowl.

prep & cook time 30 minutes **serves** 6

pesto potato
salad

1½ pounds baby new potatoes, unpeeled, quartered
½ cup mayonnaise
2 scallions, thinly sliced
¼ cup finely sliced fresh basil
2 teaspoons fresh lemon zest

basil pesto
2 tablespoons pine nuts
½ cup firmly packed fresh basil leaves
¼ cup grated Parmesan cheese
1 clove garlic, quartered
⅓ cup olive oil

1 Boil, steam or microwave potato until tender; drain.

2 Meanwhile, make basil pesto.

3 Combine mayonnaise and pesto in large bowl; add onions and hot potato, mix gently.

4 Serve salad topped with sliced basil and lemon zest.

basil pesto Toast pine nuts in a dry skillet over medium-high heat until fragrant. Process basil, cheese, nuts and garlic until chopped finely. With motor operating, gradually add oil in a thin, steady stream; process until almost smooth.

prep & cook time 30 minutes **serves** 6

lemon-garlic spicy potato salad

pesto potato salad

german potato salad

2 pounds potatoes, unpeeled,
  cut into 1-inch cubes
½ pound sliced bacon
½ red onion, thinly sliced
1 teaspoon black mustard seeds
⅔ cup finely chopped fresh flat-leaf parsley

sweet Dijon dressing
¼ cup cider vinegar
¼ cup olive oil
1 tablespoon Dijon mustard
½ teaspoon sugar

1 Boil, steam or microwave potato until tender; drain.

2 Meanwhile, place ingredients for sweet Dijon dressing in screw-top jar; shake well.

3 Cook bacon in a skillet over medium heat until crisp; transfer bacon to a plate lined with paper towels. Drain skillet; reserve about 1 tablespoon bacon drippings. Cook onion in same pan, stirring, until softened. Add mustard seeds; cook, stirring, 1 minute.

4 Combine potato, onion mixture, parsley and dressing in large bowl. Crumble bacon over top and toss to coat.

prep & cook time 30 minutes **serves** 6

grilled potato salad with artichoke hearts

2 pounds fingerling potatoes, halved lengthways
1 tablespoon olive oil
6 cloves garlic, halved
1 (14-ounces) can artichoke hearts, drained, quartered
1 cup firmly packed fresh flat-leaf parsley leaves

creamy mustard dressing
1 tablespoon balsamic vinegar
1 tablespoon Dijon mustard
½ cup (125ml) light cream

1 Place ingredients for creamy mustard dressing in screw-top jar; shake well.

2 Boil, steam or microwave potato until tender; drain. Combine potato and oil in medium bowl.

3 Place an oiled grill plate over medium-high heat. Cook potato, garlic and artichoke, in batches until potato is browned.

4 Return vegetables to same bowl with parsley; toss gently to combine. Serve salad drizzled with dressing.

prep & cook time 25 minutes **serves** 4

german potato salad

grilled potato salad with artichoke hearts

cabbage, orange & radish salad

1 orange
2 cups finely shredded green cabbage
2 red radishes, trimmed, thinly sliced
½ cup loosely packed fresh mint

cumin and orange dressing
1 teaspoon cumin seeds
¼ teaspoon hot paprika
2 tablespoons olive oil
1 tablespoon white balsamic vinegar

1 Segment orange over small bowl; reserve 1 tablespoon juice for dressing.

2 Make cumin and orange dressing.

3 Place orange segments and dressing in large bowl with remaining ingredients; toss gently to combine.

cumin and orange dressing Toast spices in dry skillet over medium heat until fragrant; cool. Place spices in screw-top jar with oil, vinegar and reserved orange juice; shake well.

prep & cook time 25 minutes   **serves** 4

warm red cabbage & bacon salad

1¼ pound sliced bacon, coarsely chopped
1 tablespoon olive oil
6 cups coarsely shredded red cabbage
2 tablespoons red wine vinegar
1 tablespoon brown sugar
½ cup coarsely chopped fresh flat-leaf parsley

1 Cook bacon in a skillet over medium heat until crisp. Transfer bacon to a plate lined with paper towels. Drain skillet, reserve about 1 teaspoon bacon drippings.

2 Heat oil in same skillet; cook cabbage, stirring, about 5 minutes or until softened. Add vinegar and sugar; cook, stirring, about 10 minutes or until liquid evaporates.

3 Return bacon to skillet; cook, stirring, until heated through. Remove from heat; stir in parsley.

prep & cook time 25 minutes   **serves** 4

cabbage, orange & radish salad

warm red cabbage & bacon salad

winter vegetable coleslaw

2 cups finely shredded cabbage
1 baby fennel bulb, trimmed, thinly sliced
¼ pound green beans, trimmed, thinly sliced
1 pound celeriac, peeled, coarsely grated
1 stalk celery, trimmed, thinly sliced
1 cup loosely packed fresh flat-leaf parsley

cider dressing
¼ cup olive oil
2 tablespoons cider vinegar
1 teaspoon sugar
1 teaspoon Dijon mustard

1 Place ingredients for cider dressing in screw-top jar; shake well.

2 Place cabbage and fennel in large bowl with remaining salad ingredients and dressing; toss gently to combine.

prep time 25 minutes **serves** 4

coleslaw

½ small cabbage, finely shredded
1 carrot, coarsely grated
4 scallions, thinly sliced
½ cup mayonnaise
1 tablespoon lemon juice

1 Combine vegetables, mayonnaise and juice in large bowl.

prep time 10 minutes **serves** 6

winter vegetable coleslaw

coleslaw

vegetarian salads

tabbouleh

¼ cup fine bulgur
3 tomatoes
3 cups coarsely chopped fresh flat-leaf parsley
3 scallions, finely chopped
½ cup coarsely chopped fresh mint
1 clove garlic, crushed
¼ cup lemon juice
¼ cup olive oil

1 Place bulgur in shallow medium bowl. Halve tomatoes, scoop pulp from tomato over bulgur. Chop tomato flesh finely; spread over bulgur. Cover; refrigerate 1 hour.

2 Place bulgur mixture in large bowl with remaining ingredients; stir to combine.

prep time 30 minutes (+ refrigeration)   **serves** 4

Perfect tabbouleh relies on perfect parsley: it's imperative that the parsley is well washed to remove any grit and dried thoroughly before adding to the salad. If the parsley is too wet, you will find that your tabbouleh turns a little mushy, rather than being light and tasty.

green bean & tomato salad

½ pound green beans, trimmed
1 pint cherry tomatoes, halved

mustard hazelnut dressing
½ cup hazelnuts
2 tablespoons hazelnut oil
2 tablespoons cider vinegar
1 teaspoon wholegrain mustard

1 Toast hazelnuts in a dry skillet over medium-high heat until fragrant and skins of hazelnuts start to split. Transfer to a plate to cool; peel by rubbing of skins with fingers or a kitchen towel. Chop coarsely.

2 Place ingredients for mustard hazelnut dressing in screw-top jar; shake well.

3 Boil, steam or microwave beans until tender; drain. Rinse under cold water; drain.

4 Place beans and dressing in medium bowl with tomatoes; toss gently to combine.

prep & cook time 20 minutes **serves** 4

arugula & parmesan salad

2 tablespoons pine nuts
1 tablespoon balsamic vinegar
1 tablespoon olive oil
5 ounces baby arugula
½ cup oil-packed sun-dried tomatoes, drained and coarsely chopped
⅓ cup shaved parmesan

1 Toast remaining pine nuts in a dry skillet over medium-high heat until fragnant.

2 Place ingredients in large bowl; toss gently to combine.

prep time 10 minutes **serves** 4

green bean & tomato salad

arugula & parmesan salad

rainbow salad

1¼ pounds baby beets, trimmed
½ pounds asparagus, trimmed
2 cloves garlic, crushed
1 tablespoon fresh lemon zest
2 small avocados, cut into thin wedges
3 oranges, segmented
1 red onion, thinly sliced

wholegrain mustard dressing
1 tablespoon wholegrain mustard
1 tablespoon cider vinegar
1 tablespoon finely chopped fresh chives
¼ cup coarsely chopped fresh flat-leaf parsley

1 Preheat oven to 350°F (325°F convection).

2 Place beets on baking sheet; roast uncovered, about 45 minutes or until beets is tender. Cool 10 minutes. Peel beets; cut in quarters.

3 Meanwhile, combine asparagus, garlic and zest on baking sheet; roast, uncovered, about 10 minutes or until asparagus is tender. Cut asparagus in half, crossways.

4 Combine ingredients for wholegrain mustard dressing in small bowl.

5 Place beets and asparagus mixture in large bowl with remaining ingredients and dressing; toss gently to combine.

prep & cook time 1 hour **serves** 4

eggplant, tomato & parsley salad

2 large eggplants (1 pound each), cut into
½ inch slices
2 large tomatoes, chopped finely
1 cup coarsely chopped fresh flat-leaf parsley

mint yogurt dressing
½ cup low-fat plain yogurt
2 tablespoons water
1 tablespoon finely chopped fresh mint

1 Place a lightly oiled grill plate over medium-high heat. Cook eggplant in batches, about 2 minutes each side, until tender.

2 Meanwhile, combine ingredients for mint yogurt dressing in small bowl.

3 Divide eggplant, tomato and parsley among serving plates; drizzle with dressing.

prep & cook time 20 minutes   **serves** 4

panzanella with radish sandwiches

4 slices white bread, crusts removed
4 teaspoons butter, softened
4 red radishes, trimmed, thinly sliced
1 avocado, halved, coarsely chopped
1 can (15 ounces) butter beans, rinsed, drained
4 tomatoes, coarsely chopped
1 yellow bell pepper, coarsely chopped
1 English cucumber, coarsely chopped
1 cup firmly packed fresh basil

tomato dressing
1 large tomato, peeled seeded
¼ cup olive oil
1 tablespoon white balsamic vinegar
½ teaspoon sugar

1   Spread bread with butter; top two slices with radish, top with remaining bread. Using rolling pin, gently flatten radish sandwiches. Cut sandwiches into small squares.

2   Make tomato dressing.

3   Combine avocado and remaining ingredients with the dressing in large bowl. Divide salad among serving plates; top with radish sandwiches.

tomato dressing Blend or process tomato until smooth. Add remaining ingredients; pulse until combined.

prep time 30 minutes   **serves** 8

To peel the tomato for the dressing, cut a shallow cross in the bottom of the tomato and put it into a bowl of just-boiled water for about 1 minute. The skin should then peel away easily. Cut the peeled tomato in half, then scoop out the seeds using a teaspoon.

goat cheese & fig salad

6 slices prosciutto (optional)
5 ounces baby arugula, trimmed
4 large fresh figs, quartered
4 ounces soft goat cheese, crumbled

honey cider dressing
¼ cup cider vinegar
2 tablespoons olive oil
1 tablespoon wholegrain mustard
1 tablespoon honey

1 Preheat broiler.

2 Place ingredients for honey cider dressing in screw-top jar; shake well.

3 Crisp prosciutto under broiler; drain, chop coarsely.

4 Serve arugula topped with fig, cheese and prosciutto; drizzle with dressing.

prep & cook time 15 minutes **serves** 4

ricotta & fava bean salad

1 pound frozen fava beans
½ pound asparagus, trimmed, halved crossways
1 can (14-ounces) whole baby beets, drained, quartered
½ cup loosely packed fresh flat-leaf parsley
½ cup loosely packed fresh mint
¼ cup low-fat ricotta cheese, crumbled

hazelnut oil dressing
1 tablespoon white wine vinegar
1 teaspoon hazelnut oil
½ teaspoon white sugar

1 Cook fava beans in large saucepan of boiling water about 3 minutes or until tender, drain; rinse under cold water, drain.

2 Boil, steam or microwave asparagus until almost tender, drain; rinse under cold water, drain.

3 Place ingredients for hazelnut oil dressing in screw-top jar; shake well.

4 Place beans and asparagus in large bowl with beets, parsley and mint; toss gently to combine. Serve topped with cheese; drizzle with dressing.

prep & cook time 30 minutes **serves** 4

goat cheese & fig salad

ricotta & fava bean salad

broiled goat cheese salad

½ cup coarsely chopped walnuts
⅓ cup coarsely chopped fresh flat-leaf parsley
1 clove garlic, chopped finely
2 tablespoons walnut oil
1 tablespoon white wine vinegar
1 small Loaf French bread (5 ounces), thinly sliced
2 tablespoons olive oil
1 (9 ounces) log goat cheese, cut into 4 slices
3 ounces mesclun

1 Toast nuts in a dry skillet over medium-high heat until fragrant. Combine nuts, parsley, garlic, walnut oil and vinegar in small bowl.

2 Preheat broiler. Brush bread with olive oil and arrange on a baking sheet. Broil 1-2 minutes per side until lightly browned.

3 Place cheese slices on another baking tray. Broil until browned lightly.

4 Divide mesclun among serving plates; top with cheese and walnut mixture, serve with bread.

prep & cook time 20 minutes **serves** 4

root vegetable salad with lemon & feta

1 pound baby new potatoes, unpeeled, halved
1 pound butternut squash, peeled, seeded, chopped coarsely
4 small beets, peeled
1 parsnip, quartered
¾ pound baby carrots, trimmed
1 lemon, sliced thinly
2 tablespoons olive oil
2 tablespoons butter cut into small pieces
2 tablespoons fresh oregano leaves
2 tablespoons lemon juice
1 tablespoon wholegrain mustard
5 ounces baby arugula
4 ounces feta, crumbled

1 Preheat oven to 400°F (375°F convection).

2 Combine potato, squash, beets, parsnip, carrots, lemon, oil, butter and half the oregano in large shallow baking dish. Roast, uncovered, turning occasionally, about 40 minutes or until vegetables are tender.

3 Meanwhile, place juice and mustard in screw-top jar; shake well.

4 Place vegetables in large bowl with mustard mixture and arugula; toss gently to combine. Sprinkle cheese and remaining oregano on top.

prep & cook time 50 minutes   **serves** 4

eggplant, feta & sun-dried tomato salad

2 red bell peppers
8 baby eggplants (about 1 pound), halved lengthways
1 red onion, cut into wedges
8 ounces feta cheese, crumbled
10 ounces watercress
½ cup oil-packed sun-dried tomatoes, drained and thinly sliced

creamy horseradish dressing
1 egg
2 teaspoons honey
2 tablespoons prepared horseradish
2 cloves garlic, quartered
⅔ cup olive oil

1 Quarter bell peppers; discard seeds and membranes. Cook bell peppers, eggplant and onion, in batches, until browned. Transfer bell pepper pieces to a glass bowl. Cover for 5 minutes to allow steam to loosen their skins; peel.

2 Make creamy horseradish dressing.

3 Combine cheese, watercress and tomato in medium bowl; divide among serving plates. Top with bell peppers, eggplant and onion; drizzle with dressing.

creamy horseradish dressing Blend or process egg, honey, horseradish and garlic until smooth. With motor operating, add oil in thin, steady stream until dressing thickens slightly.

prep & cook time 35 minutes   **serves** 6

root vegetable salad with lemon & feta

eggplant, feta & sun-dried tomato salad

roasted squash, carrot & parsnip salad

1 (1 pound) butternut squash, peeled, seeded, sliced
1 tablespoon olive oil
4 large carrots, halved, sliced thickly
2 large parsnips, chopped coarsely
⅓ cup firmly packed fresh flat-leaf parsley
¼ cup pine nuts

spice glaze
2 cloves garlic, quartered
1 teaspoon cumin seeds
1 teaspoon coriander seeds
½ teaspoon ground cinnamon
1 teaspoon sea salt
1 tablespoon olive oil
1 tablespoon butter
¼ cup firmly packed brown sugar
1½ cups apple juice

1 Preheat oven to 400°F (375°F convection).

2 Place squash and oil in large baking dish; toss squash to coat. Roast, uncovered, about 25 minutes or until just tender.

3 Meanwhile, boil, steam or microwave carrot and parsnip, separately, until just tender; drain. Make spice glaze. Toastpine nuts in a dry skillet over medium-high heat until fragrant.

4 Place vegetables, parsley and nuts in large bowl with spice mixture; toss gently to combine.

spice glaze Using mortar and pestle or small electric spice blender, crush garlic, cumin, coriander, cinnamon, salt and oil until mixture forms a thick paste. Melt butter in large skillet; cook paste, stirring, about 3 minutes or until fragrant. Add sugar and juice; bring to the boil. Cook, stirring, about 10 minutes or until spice mixture thickens slightly.

prep & cook time 40 minutes   **serves** 8

raw squash, pomegranate & pepita salad

1 pound piece butternut squash, peeled
½ cup pomegranate seeds
4 cups baby spinach
1 tablespoon pepitas

red wine vinegar dressing
2 tablespoons olive oil
2 teaspoon red wine vinegar
1 teaspoon dijon mustard

1 Using mandolin or V-slicer, cut squash into paper-thin slices.

2 Place ingredients for red wine vinegar dressing in screw-top jar; shake well.

3 Place squash and dressing in large bowl with pomegranate and spinach; toss gently to combine. Serve salad sprinkled with pepitas.

prep time 15 minutes **serves** 4

warm squash & zucchini salad with leek dressing

8 medium yellow patty-pan squash, quartered
12 baby zucchini

leek dressing
2 teaspoons olive oil
1 small leek, thinly sliced
2 tablespoons lemon juice
1 tablespoon vegetable stock
1 tablespoon rice vinegar
2 teaspoons lemon thyme leaves

1 Make leek dressing.

2 Meanwhile, cook squash and zucchini in a covered steamer basket, set over a saucepan of simmering water, about 5 minutes or until tender.

3 Serve vegetables drizzled with leek dressing.

leek dressing Heat oil in small skillet; cook leek, stirring, about 10 minutes or until tender. Remove from heat; stir in remaining ingredients.

prep & cook time 15 minutes **serves** 4

mixed vegetable salad with baba ghanoush

1 large green bell pepper
1 large red bell pepper
1 large yellow bell pepper
1 large eggplant
2 cloves garlic, unpeeled
1 tablespoon lemon juice
1 tablespoon tahini
½ cup olive oil
¾ pound portabello caps mushroom, thickly sliced
1 sprig fresh thyme
1 pint cherry tomatoes
20 baby zucchini, halved
8 yellow patty-pan squash, halved
2 small fennel bulbs trimmed, quartered
12 shallots, peeled
⅓ cup dry white wine
1 long loaf Turkish bread or other flat bread
½ cup loosely packed fresh flat-leaf parsley

1 Preheat oven to 475°F (450°F convection).

2 Quarter bell peppers, discard seeds and membranes. Using fork, prick eggplant all over; place on oiled baking sheet with garlic and peppers, skin-side up. Roast vegetables, uncovered, about 30 minutes or until skins blister. Transfer bell pepper pieces to a glass bowl. Cover for 5 minutes to allow steam to loosen their skins; peel.

3 When cool enough to handle, peel eggplant and garlic. Blend or process eggplant, garlic, juice and tahini until mixture forms a paste. With motor operating, pour in half of the oil in a thin, steady stream until eggplant mixture is pureed. Reserve.

4 Meanwhile, toss mushrooms and thyme with 1 tablespoon of the remaining oil in large shallow baking dish. Toss tomatoes, zucchini, squash and 1 tablespoon of the remaining oil in another large shallow baking dish. Roast, uncovered, about 20 minutes or until mushrooms and vegetables are just tender.

5 Heat remaining oil in medium saucepan; cook fennel and shallots, stirring occasionally, about 5 minutes or until vegetables are lightly browned. Add wine; cook, covered, about 20 minutes or until vegetables are tender, stirring occasionally. Drain vegetables; add cooking liquid to processor with eggplant puree, process until smooth. This mixture is the baba ghanoush.

6 Quarter bread; slice quarters horizontally. Place an oiled grill plate over medium-high heat. Cook bread until lightly browned on both sides. Divide bread among serving plates; top with combined mushrooms, vegetables and parsley. Serve with baba ghanoush.

prep & cook time 1 hour 50 minutes **serves** 4

char-grilled vegetable salad

1 medium red bell pepper
1 medium yellow bell pepper
1 large red onion, halved, cut into wedges
1 small sweet potato, sliced thinly lengthways
2 baby eggplants, sliced thinly lengthways
2 zucchini (about ½ pound), halved lengthways
1 can (14 ounces) jar artichoke hearts,
   drained, halved
½ cup seeded kalamata olives
1 small radicchio, trimmed, leaves separated

oregano dressing
¼ cup olive oil
2 tablespoons red wine vinegar
2 tablespoons lemon juice
2 cloves garlic, crushed
1 tablespoon finely chopped fresh oregano

1   Quarter bell peppers, remove and discard seeds and membranes; cut peppers into thick strips.

2   Place ingredients for oregano dressing in screw-top jar; shake well.

3   Place an oiled grill plate over medium-light heat. Cook bell peppers, in batches, until browned and tender. Cook onion, sweet potato, eggplant, zucchini and artichoke, in batches, until browned.

4   Place char-grilled vegetables, olives and dressing in large bowl; toss gently to combine. Serve vegetables with radicchio.

prep & cook time 55 minutes   **serves** 4

greek salad with marinated feta

2 tomatoes
1 cucumber
1 small red bell pepper
1 small red onion, thinly sliced
1 cup pitted black olives

marinated feta
8 ounces feta, cut into ½ inch pieces
1 fresh long red chili, chopped finely
2 teaspoons finely grated lemon rind
2 tablespoons fresh oregano leaves
1 cup olive oil

1 Make marinated feta.

2 Halve and seed tomatoes, cucumber and bell pepper; cut vegetables into matchstick size pieces.

3 Place a third of the marinated feta and a third of the oil marinade in large bowl with tomato, cucumber, bell pepper, onion and olives; toss gently to combine.

marinated feta cheese Place cheese in sterilized glass jar. Combine remaining ingredients in a large measuring cup; pour over cheese. Refrigerate 3 hours or overnight. Store leftover feta in the refrigerator, for up to four weeks.

prep time 25 minutes (+ refrigeration) **serves** 6

greek-style wild rice salad

2 cups wild rice blend
½ cup pine nuts
1 red bell pepper
1 onion, quartered
1 pint cherry tomatoes
¾ pound broccolini, halved crossways
1 cup coarsely chopped fresh flat-leaf parsley
2 tablespoons lemon juice

lemon and garlic yogurt
2 cloves garlic, crushed
1 cup plain yogurt
¼ cup lemon juice

1 Combine ingredients for lemon and garlic yogurt in small bowl.

2 Cook rice according to package instructions. Place in large serving bowl.

3 Toast pine nuts in a dry skillet over medium-high heat until fragrant.

4 Quarter bell peppers; discard seeds and membranes. Place an oiled grill plate over medium-high heat. Cook bell peppers, onion and tomatoes until tender. Chop peppers and onion coarsely.

5 Boil, steam or microwave broccolini until tender.

6 Add bell peppers, onion and tomatoes to bowl of rice with nuts, parsley and juice; stir gently to combine. Serve salad topped with broccolini, then yogurt.

prep & cook time 35 minutes **serves** 4

greek salad with marinated feta

greek-style wild rice salad

bean, pasta & grain salads

fattoush

6 pocket pita (about 1 pound)
  olive oil, for frying
3 tomatoes, coarsely chopped
1 large green bell pepper, coarsely chopped
2 cucumbers, seeded, thinly sliced
10 trimmed red radishes, thinly sliced
4 spring onions, thinly sliced
1½ cups firmly packed fresh flat-leaf parsley
½ cup coarsely chopped fresh mint

lemon garlic dressing
2 cloves garlic, crushed
¼ cup olive oil
¼ cup lemon juice

1 Halve pita horizontally; cut into 1-inch piece. Heat about ¼ oil in wok or large deep skillet; fry pita, in batches, until lightly browned and crisp. Drain on towels.

2 Place ingredients for lemon garlic dressing in screw-top jar; shake well.

3 Just before serving, place about three-quarters of the pita in large bowl with dressing and remaining ingredients; toss gently to combine. Sprinkle remaining pita over fattoush.

prep & cook time 35 minutes **serves** 4

fennel & tomato couscous salad

1 pint cherry tomatoes, halved
1 cup couscous
1 cup boiling water
2 baby fennel bulbs (about ½ pound), trimmed, sliced thinly
¼ cup olive oil
1 tablespoon white wine vinegar
1 clove garlic, crushed
2 tablespoons finely chopped fresh oregano

1 Preheat oven to 400°F (375°F convection). Place tomatoes on rimmed baking sheet lined with parchment paper. Roast 10 minutes or until skins burst.

2 Meanwhile, combine couscous with the water in medium heatproof bowl, cover; stand about 5 minutes or until water is absorbed, fluffing with fork occasionally.

3 Stir tomato and remaining ingredients into couscous.

prep & cook time 20 minutes **serves** 4

couscous salad with chickpeas

1½ cups couscous
1½ cups boiling water
1 tablespoon butter
⅓ cup pine nuts
1 can (15 ounces) chickpeas, rinsed, drained
⅓ cup raisins or dried currants
5 ounces baby arugula, coarsely chopped
¾ cup finely chopped fresh flat-leaf parsley
1 cup pitted green olives

lemon dressing
1 tablespoon fresh lemon zest
¼ cup lemon juice
¼ cup olive oil
2 tablespoons rinsed and drained finely chopped preserved lemon (optional)

1 Combine couscous with the water in large heatproof bowl, cover; stand about 5 minutes or until water is absorbed, fluffing with fork occasionally. Stir in butter. Stand 10 minutes.

2 Toast pine nuts in a dry skillet over medium-high heat until fragrant.

3 Place ingredients for preserved lemon dressing in screw-top jar; shake well.

4 Place couscous in large bowl with remaining ingredients and dressing; toss gently to combine.

prep time 20 minutes **serves** 4

fennel & tomato couscous salad

couscous salad with chickpeas

curried couscous & chickpea salad

½ cup water
½ cup chicken stock
1 teaspoon curry powder
1 cup couscous
1 (15 ounces) can chickpeas, rinsed, drained
½ cup crumbled feta
½ cup coarsely chopped fresh coriander
2 scallions, thinly sliced
1 teaspoon fresh lemon zest
¼ cup lemon juice

1 Bring the water, stock and curry powder to a boil in small saucepan.

2 Combine couscous in medium heatproof bowl with stock mixture, cover; stand about 5 minutes or until water is absorbed, fluffing with fork occasionally.

3 Stir remaining ingredients into couscous.

prep & cook time 15 minutes   **serves** 4

orange & date couscous salad

1 cup couscous
1 cup boiling water
2 medium oranges
1 cup baby spinach leaves
½ small red onion, sliced thinly
½ cup pitted dates, sliced thinly
1 tablespoon olive oil

1 Combine couscous with the water in medium heatproof bowl, cover; stand about 5 minutes or until water is absorbed, fluffing with fork occasionally.

2 Meanwhile, coarsely grate zest from both oranges. Segment oranges over small bowl; reserve any juice in bowl (you need ¼ cup juice). Stir orange segments, reserved juice and remaining ingredients into couscous.

prep time 15 minutes   **serves** 4

curried couscous & chickpea salad

orange & date couscous salad

vegetable & couscous salad

1 sweet potato cut into thin slices
2 large zucchini (about ½ pound), cut into thin slices
1½ cups couscous
1½ cups hot chicken stock
1 can (14 ounces) whole baby beets, drained, quartered
1 cup baby spinach leaves
2 tablespoons coarsely chopped fresh flat-leaf parsley

orange dressing
1 teaspoon fresh orange zest
¼ cup orange juice
2 tablespoons white wine vinegar
1 teaspoon Dijon mustard

1 Place an oiled grill plate over medium-high heat. Cook sweet potato in batches, until tender. Cool 10 minutes.

2 Meanwhile, combine couscous with stock in large heatproof bowl, cover; stand 5 minutes or until liquid is absorbed, fluffing with fork occasionally.

3 Place ingredients for orange dressing in screw-top jar; shake well.

4 Add sweet potato zucchini and remaining ingredients to couscous; stir gently to combine. Serve salad drizzled with dressing.

prep & cook time 20 minutes **serves** 4

chili, corn, tomato & chickpea salad

1 can chipotle chili adobo sauce
½ cup crushed tomatoes
1 tablespoon lime juice
1 teaspoon ground cumin
2 trimmed corn cobs
1 can (15 ounces) chickpeas, drained, rinsed
1 pint cherry tomatoes, halved
1 small red onion, thinly sliced
1 cup loosely packed fresh cilantro

1   Mash chili in small bowl; add tomatoes and juice. Blend or process until mixture is smooth.

2   Toast cumin in a dry skillet over medium-high heat, stirring, until fragrant; stir into chili sauce mixture.

3   Place an oiled grill plate over medium-high heat. Cook corn until browned lightly and tender. Cut kernels from cobs.

4   Combine chili mixture and corn in large bowl with remaining ingredients.

prep & cook time 35 minutes (+ standing)   **serves** 4

crispy polenta salad

- 4 cups water
- 1 cup polenta
- ½ cup grated parmesan cheese
- ½ cup grated Cheddar cheese
- 1 tablespoon olive oil
- 4 cups baby spinach leaves
- 1 large red bell pepper, thinly sliced
- 1 small red onion, thinly sliced

walnut dressing
- ⅓ cup coarsely chopped walnuts
- ¼ cup walnut oil
- 2 tablespoons white wine vinegar
- 1 clove garlic, crushed
- ¼ cup coarsely chopped fresh flat-leaf parsley

1 Oil 9 x 13 baking pan.

2 Bring the water to the boil in medium saucepan. Gradually stir in polenta; reduce heat. Simmer, stirring, about 10 minutes or until polenta thickens. Stir in cheeses; spread polenta into pan. Refrigerate 1 hour or until firm.

3 Meanwhile, toast walnuts in a dry skillet over medium-high heat until fragrant. Place with remaining ingredients for walnut dressing in screw-top jar; shake well.

4 Turn polenta onto board; cut into quarters then cut into ½ inch cubes. Heat oil in large skillet; cook polenta until lightly browned.

5 Place polenta in large bowl with remaining ingredients and dressing; toss gently to combine.

prep & cook time 25 minutes (+ refrigeration)
serves 4

split pea salad with mustard dressing

- ½ cup yellow split peas
- ½ cup green split peas
- 4 scallions, thinly sliced
- 1 pint cherry tomatoes, halved
- ½ cup coarsely chopped fresh flat-leaf parsley

mustard dressing
- ¼ cup lemon juice
- ¼ cup olive oil
- 1 tablespoon wholegrain mustard
- 2 cloves garlic, crushed

1 Place peas in medium bowl, cover with cold water; stand overnight, drain. Rinse under cold water; drain.

2 Place peas in medium saucepan, cover with boiling water. Simmer, covered, about 10 minutes or until peas are tender; rinse under cold water, drain.

3 Whisk ingredients for mustard dressing in small bowl.

4 Combine peas in large bowl with remaining ingredients and dressing; mix gently.

prep & cook time 30 minutes (+ standing)   **serves** 6

crispy polenta salad

split pea salad with mustard dressing

lentil & goat cheese salad

- 1 red bell pepper, thickly sliced
- 2 tablespoons extra virgin olive oil
- ½ cup French lentils, rinsed, drained
- 1 onion, halved
- 1 bay leaf
- 16 sprigs fresh thyme
- 9 ounces firm goat cheese
- 2 tablespoons packaged breadcrumbs
- 2 teaspoons fresh lemon zest
- 1 tablespoon coarsely chopped fresh flat-leaf parsley
- 1 pint cherry tomatoes, halved
- 5 ounces mesclun

vinaigrette
- 1 tablespoon red wine vinegar
- 2 tablespoons extra virgin olive oil
- 1 teaspoon Dijon mustard
- 1 teaspoon sugar

1 Preheat oven to 475°F (450°F convection).

2 Combine bell pepper and half of the oil in large shallow baking dish. Roast, uncovered, about 15 minutes or until bell pepper just softens.

3 Meanwhile, combine lentils, onion, bay leaf and thyme in medium saucepan, cover with water; bring to the boil. Reduce heat; simmer, covered, about 20 minutes or until lentils just tender. Drain; discard onion, bay leaf and thyme.

4 Meanwhile, place ingredients for vinaigrette in screw-top jar; shake well.

5 Cut cheese into 16 pieces; coat cheese in breadcrumbs. Heat remaining oil in medium skillet; cook cheese, uncovered, about 5 minutes or until cheese is lightly browned and starting to melt.

6 Meanwhile, combine lentils in medium bowl with zest, parsley, tomato and two-thirds of the vinaigrette. Divide lentils among serving plates; top with bell pepper, mesclun then cheese, drizzle with remaining vinaigrette.

prep & cook time 1 hour 10 minutes   **serves** 4

sweet potato & rice salad

1 cup brown rice
1 small sweet potato, coarsely chopped
1 pint red grape tomatoes, halved
2 scallions, thinly sliced
⅓ cup coarsely chopped fresh basil
2 cups baby arugula

balsamic dressing
2 tablespoons orange juice
1 tablespoon balsamic vinegar
1 teaspoon olive oil
1 clove garlic, crushed

1 Place and oiled grill plate over medium-high heat. Cook rice according to package instructions; drain. Rinse under cold water; drain.

2 Meanwhile, boil, steam or microwave sweet potato until tender; drain.

3 Place ingredients for balsamic dressing in screw-top jar; shake well.

4 Place rice and sweet potato in large bowl with remaining ingredients and dressing; toss gently to combine.

prep & cook time 30 minutes **serves** 4

lentil, zucchini & chorizo salad

½ cup lentils, rinsed, drained
1 onion, halved
1 bay leaf
2 chorizo sausages (5 ounces each), thinly sliced
1 zucchini (about ¼ pound), thinly sliced lengthways
1 pint red grape tomatoes, halved
1 cup loosely packed fresh flat-leaf parsley

Cajun dressing
¼ cup olive oil
1 tablespoon red wine vinegar
2 tablespoons Cajun spice mix

1 Combine lentils, onion and bay leaf in a medium sauce saucepan and cover with water; bring to a boil, reduce heat; simmer, covered about 20 minutes or until lentils are tender.

2 Cook chorizo and zucchini on heated oiled grill plate (or grill or barbecue) until chorizo is cooked and zucchini is tender.

3 Meanwhile, place ingredients for cajun dressing in screw-top jar; shake well.

4 Place chorizo and zucchini in large bowl with dressing and remaining ingredients; toss gently to combine.

prep & cook time 1hr 10 minutes **serves** 4

sweet potato & rice salad

lentil, zucchini & chorizo salad

tomato tapenade pasta salad

1 pound rotini pasta
1 pint cherry tomatoes, halved
2 cups baby arugula
⅓ cup grated Parmesan cheese

tomato tapenade
½ cup drained sun-dried tomatoes in oil
½ cup pitted black olives
2 tablespoons olive oil
1 tablespoon red wine vinegar
2 teaspoons brown sugar

1 Cook pasta in large saucepan of boiling water until tender; drain. Rinse under cold water; drain.

2 Meanwhile, make tomato tapenade.

3 Place pasta and tapenade in large bowl with remaining ingredients; toss gently to combine.

tomato tapenade Blend or process ingredients until smooth.

prep & cook time 20 minutes **serves** 6

italian brown rice salad

3 cups vegetable stock
2 teaspoons olive oil
1 small onion, finely chopped
1½ cups brown medium-grain rice
1 teaspoon fresh lime zest
1 clove garlic, crushed
⅓ cup slivered almonds
⅔ cup sun-dried tomatoes, coarsely chopped
½ cup pitted black olives, coarsely chopped
½ cup coarsely chopped fresh basil
¼ cup chopped fresh flat-leaf parsley (optional)

lime and mustard dressing
2 tablespoons lime juice
2 tablespoons white wine vinegar
2 cloves garlic, crushed
2 teaspoons Dijon mustard

1 Place stock in medium saucepan; bring to the boil. Reduce heat; simmer, covered.

2 Meanwhile, heat oil in large saucepan; cook onion, stirring, until soft. Add rice, zest and garlic; stir to coat rice in onion mixture.

3 Add stock; bring to the boil. Reduce heat; simmer, covered, about 50 minutes or until rice is tender and liquid is absorbed.

4 Toast almonds in a dry skillet over medium-high heat until fragrant.

5 Place ingredients for lime and mustard dressing in screw-top jar; shake well.

6 Add remaining ingredients and dressing to rice mixture in pan; toss gently to combine.

7 Serve salad warm; top with fresh flat-leaf parsley, if desired.

prep & cook time 1 hour 15 minutes **serves** 4

tomato tapenade pasta salad

italian brown rice salad

mexican bean salad with tortilla chips

4 tomatoes, seeded, coarsely chopped
1 can (15 ounces) small red beans, rinsed, drained
1 can (15 ounces) kidney beans, rinsed, drained
½ cup coarsely chopped fresh cilantro
¼ cup lime juice
1 small red onion, finely chopped
2 fresh long red chilies, finely chopped
4 small flour tortillas, cut into wedges
1 small avocado
2 tablespoons light sour cream

1 Preheat oven to 400°F (375°F convection).

2 Combine tomatoes, beans, ⅓ cup of the cilantro, 1 tablespoon of the juice, half of the onion and half of the chilies in medium bowl.

3 Place tortilla wedges, in single layer, on baking sheet; toast about 5 minutes or until crisp.

4 Meanwhile, to make guacamole, mash avocado in small bowl; stir in remaining cilantro, juice, onion and chili.

5 Divide tortilla chips among plates; top with bean mixture, guacamole and sour cream.

prep & cook time 25 minutes   **serves** 4

cannellini beans & olives with arugula

1 can (15 ounces) cannellini beans, rinsed, drained
1 red onion, finely chopped
⅔ cup drained, sun-dried tomatoes, chopped
8 ounces mozzarella cheese, cut into ½-inch pieces
½ cup pitted kalamata olives
5 ounces arugula

oregano balsamic vinaigrette
1 clove garlic, crushed
1 tablespoon finely chopped fresh oregano
¼ cup balsamic vinegar
¼ cup extra virgin olive oil

1 Place ingredients for oregano balsamic vinaigrette in screw-top jar; shake well.

2 Place beans, onion, tomatoes, cheese and olives in medium bowl with vinaigrette; toss gently to combine.

3 Serve bean mixture with arugula.

prep time 20 minutes   **serves** 4

ricotta & zucchini pasta salad

1 pound penne pasta
4 large zucchini (about 1 pound), thinly sliced lengthways
⅓ cup olive oil
1 tablespoon fresh lemon zest
⅓ cup lemon juice
2 cloves garlic, crushed
1 container (15 ounces) ricotta cheese, crumbled
½ cup loosely packed fresh basil leaves, finely shredded

1 Cook pasta in large saucepan of boiling water until tender; drain.

2 Meanwhile, combine zucchini and half the oil in medium bowl. Cook zucchini, in batches, on heated oiled grill plate (or grill or barbecue) until tender.

3 Combine zucchini, rind, juice, garlic and remaining oil in large bowl. Add pasta, cheese and basil; toss gently to combine.

prep & cook time 25 minutes   **serves** 6

cannellini beans & olives with arugula

ricotta & zucchini pasta salad

pasta & garlic salad

1 pound farfalle pasta
¼ cup olive oil
6 tablespoons butter
2½ cups stale breadcrumbs
4 cloves garlic, crushed
1 cup coarsely chopped fresh flat-leaf parsley

1 Cook pasta in large saucepan of boiling water until tender; drain.

2 Meanwhile, heat oil and butter in large skillet; cook breadcrumbs and garlic over medium heat, stirring, until breadcrumbs brown.

3 Place hot pasta, breadcrumbs and parsley in large bowl; toss gently to combine.

prep & cook time 20 minutes **serves** 6

creamy tomato pasta salad

1 pound rigatoni pasta
2 teaspoons olive oil
¼ pound sliced prosciutto
1 cup crème fraîche
½ cup tomato chutney
8 ounces bocconcini, halved (small mozzarella balls)
1 small red onion, thinly sliced
1 cup loosely packed fresh basil, coarsely chopped

1 Cook pasta in large saucepan of boiling water until tender; drain. Rinse under cold water; drain.

2 Meanwhile, warm oil over medium-high heat in large frying pan, cook prosciutto until crisp. Drain on paper towels; chop coarsely.

3 Combine crème fraîche and chutney in large bowl, then add pasta, prosciutto and remaining ingredients; toss gently to combine.

prep & cook time 25 minutes **serves** 6

pasta & garlic salad

creamy tomato pasta salad

chicken & pasta salad

¾ pound large shell pasta
1 cup frozen peas
3 cups shredded cooked chicken
1 cup baby arugula

arugula pesto
2 tablespoons roasted pine nuts
1 cup baby arugula
½ cup grated Parmesan cheese
2 teaspoons fresh lemon zest
1 tablespoon lemon juice
¼ cup olive oil

1 Cook pasta in large saucepan of boiling water until tender. Add peas during last minute of pasta cooking time; drain.

2 Meanwhile, make arugula pesto.

3 Place pasta, peas and pesto in large bowl with remaining ingredients; toss gently to combine.

arugula pesto Toast pine nuts in a dry skillet over medium-high heat until fragrant. Blend or process nuts, arugula, cheese, zest and juice until finely chopped. With motor running, gradually add oil in a thin steady stream; blend until pesto is smooth.

prep & cook time 30 minutes   **serves** 4

pasta salad with brussels sprouts

1 pound rigatoni pasta
1 tablespoon olive oil
¾ pound Brussels sprouts, trimmed, shredded
½ cup coarsely chopped fresh flat-leaf parsley
1 tablespoon drained capers, rinsed
8 ounces bocconcini (small mozzarella balls), thickly sliced
½ cup smoked almonds, coarsely chopped

red wine vinaigrette
⅓ cup lemon juice
⅓ cup red wine vinegar
¼ cup olive oil
1 teaspoon white sugar
2 cloves garlic, crushed

1 Place ingredients for red wine vinaigrette in screw-top jar; shake well.

2 Cook pasta in large saucepan of boiling water, uncovered, until just tender; drain.

3 Heat oil in same pan; stir-fry sprouts about 1 minute or until just warm.

4 Place pasta and sprouts in large serving bowl with remaining ingredients and vinaigrette; toss gently to combine.

prep & cook time 35 minutes   **serves** 4

chicken & pasta salad

pasta salad with brussels sprouts

coconut chicken & noodle salad

2 large boneless chicken breasts (about 1¼ pounds)
1 cup coconut milk
1½ cups chicken stock
1 tablespoon brown sugar
1 clove garlic, crushed
1 piece (1-inch) fresh ginger, grated
1 tablespoon fish sauce
2 tablespoons lime juice
4 ounces vermicelli rice noodles
1 small carrot, sliced thinly
¼ cup drained sliced bamboo shoots, rinsed
¼ cup loosely packed fresh coriander, finely chopped
¼ cup loosely packed fresh mint, finely chopped

1 Place chicken in medium saucepan with milk, stock, sugar, garlic and ginger; bring to the boil. Reduce heat; simmer, uncovered, about 10 minutes or until cooked. Cool chicken in poaching liquid 10 minutes. Remove chicken from pan. Return poaching liquid to the boil; reduce to 1 cup. Remove from heat; stir in fish sauce and juice.

2 Meanwhile, place noodles in large heatproof bowl, cover with boiling water; stand until just tender, drain. Rinse under cold water; drain. Using scissors, cut noodles into random lengths.

3 Tear chicken coarsely. Place noodles and chicken in medium bowl with carrot and bamboo shoots; stir in poaching liquid. Serve sprinkled with herbs.

prep & cook time 50 minutes **serves** 4

asian crispy noodle salad

½ Chinese cabbage (1 pound), finely shredded
1 can (7 ounces) water chestnuts, drained, thinly sliced
¼ pound snow peas, trimmed, thinly sliced
1 large red bell pepper, thinly sliced
1 can (3 ounces) fried noodles
½ cup roasted unsalted cashews, coarsely chopped
1 cup loosely packed fresh cilantro

sesame soy dressing
1 teaspoon sesame oil
¼ cup soy sauce
1 tablespoon sweet chili sauce
2 tablespoons lime juice

1 Place ingredients for sesame soy dressing in screw-top jar; shake well.

2 Place cabbage, water chestnuts, snow peas, bell pepper and fried noodles in medium bowl; toss gently to combine.

3 Divide salad among serving bowls; sprinkle with nuts and cilantro, drizzle with dressing.

prep time 15 minutes **serves** 4

coconut chicken & noodle salad

asian crispy noodle salad

main dish salads

tuna salad

1 can (12 ounces) tuna, drained, flaked
1 small red bell pepper, finely chopped
2 scallions, thinly sliced
1 celery stalk, finely chopped
¼ cup finely chopped fresh flat-leaf parsley
2 tablespoons finely chopped fresh basil
2 tablespoons finely chopped fresh dill
½ cup mayonnaise
1 teaspoon Dijon mustard
1 teaspoon fresh lemon zest
2 teaspoons lemon juice

1 Combine tuna, bell pepper, scallions, celery and herbs in medium bowl.

2 Combine mayonnaise with remaining ingredients in small bowl.

3 Stir mayonnaise mixture into tuna mixture to combine.

prep time 20 minutes **serves** 4

potato, tuna & egg salad

6 baby new potatoes (about ½ pound)
¼ pound green beans, trimmed, halved crossways
2 tablespoons low-fat yogurt
1 teaspoon fresh lemon zest
2 teaspoons lemon juice
1 can (6 ounces) tuna, drained, flaked
3 scallions, finely sliced
1 tablespoon coarsely chopped fresh flat-leaf parsley
2 hard-boiled eggs, quartered

1 Boil, steam or microwave potatoes and beans, separately, until tender; drain, cool.

2 Meanwhile, combine yogurt, zest and juice in medium bowl.

3 Quarter potatoes; add to yogurt mixture with tuna, scallions and parsley, stir to combine. Serve salad topped with egg.

prep & cook time 20 minutes   **serves** 2

tuna, bean & haloumi salad

1 pound spinach, trimmed
½ pound haloumi cheese, cut lengthways into ½-inch slices
1 can (15 ounces) small red beans, rinsed, drained
1 can (15 ounces) small pink beans, rinsed, drained
1 can (12 ounces) tuna in oil, drained, flaked
1 pint yellow grape tomatoes, halved

creamy lemon dressing
½ cup Greek-style yogurt
½ teaspoon fresh lemon zest
1 teaspoon Dijon mustard
¼ cup lemon juice

1 Boil, steam or microwave spinach until wilted; drain, chop coarsely.

2 Meanwhile, combine ingredients for creamy lemon dressing in small bowl.

3 Cook cheese in heated oiled large skillet until lightly browned.

4 Combine spinach, beans, tuna and tomato in large bowl. Divide salad among serving bowls; top with cheese, drizzle with dressing.

prep & cook time 30 minutes   **serves** 4

potato, tuna & egg salad

tuna, bean & haloumi salad

salmon & grapefruit salad

1 piece salmon fillet (about bounces)
1 tablespoon lemon juice
½ inch piece fresh ginger, grated
½ teaspoon ground cumin
2 ruby red grapefruits
1 tablespoon white balsamic vinegar
½ teaspoon white sugar
4 cups baby spinach leaves
1½ cups bean sprouts
1 cucumber, seeded, thinly sliced

1 Combine fish in medium bowl with juice, ginger and cumin. Cook fish in small baking-paper-lined steamer, over small saucepan of simmering water, about 10 minutes. Using two forks, flake fish.

2 Meanwhile, segment grapefruits over small bowl; reserve ⅓ cup of the juice for dressing. To make dressing, place reserved juice, vinegar and sugar in screw-top jar; shake well.

3 Divide spinach, sprouts, cucumber and grapefruit segments among serving plates; top with flaked salmon and dressing.

prep & cook time 20 minutes   **serves** 4

salmon with fennel & beet salad

1 small fennel bulb, trimmed
1 beet, peeled
1 small radicchio, trimmed, finely shredded
½ cup loosely packed fresh flat-leaf parsley
1 tablespoon rice wine vinegar
¼ cup olive oil
4 salmon fillets about 6-ounces each
1½ teaspoons caraway seeds
1 clove garlic, crushed
1 lime, cut into wedges

1 Using mandolin, V-slicer or very sharp knife, slice fennel and beetroot finely. Place in large bowl with radicchio, parsley, vinegar and 2 tablespoons of the oil; toss gently to combine.

2 Combine fish, remaining oil, seeds and garlic in large bowl. Cook fish in a large skillet over medium-high heat until fish is opaque.

3 Divide salad and fish among serving plates; serve with lime.

prep & cook time 30 minutes   **serves** 4

salmon & grapefruit salad

salmon with fennel & beetroot salad

smoked salmon, orange & avocado salad

2 large oranges, segmented
2 large avocados, halved, thickly sliced
½ pound smoked salmon, skinned, flaked
4 cups baby spinach
1 cup lamb's lettuce or watercress

horseradish dressing
¼ cup orange juice
1 tablespoon olive oil
1 tablespoon white wine vinegar
1 tablespoon Greek yogurt
1 teaspoon prepared horseradish

1 Place ingredients for horseradish dressing in screw-top jar; shake well.

2 Place orange, avocado, fish, spinach and lettuce in large bowl; toss gently to combine. Divide salad among serving plates; drizzle with dressing.

prep time 15 minutes **serves** 4

shrimp & mango salad

2 pounds uncooked large shrimp
2 tablespoons light soy sauce
2 teaspoons sesame oil
1 fresh long red chili, finely chopped
1 piece (½ inch) fresh ginger, grated
2 cloves garlic, crushed
1 mango, thinly sliced
1 large red bell pepper, thinly sliced
1 cucumber, seeded, thinly sliced
1 cup bean sprouts
½ cup loosely packed fresh cilantro
2 scallions, thinly sliced

lime dressing
⅓ cup lime juice
1 tablespoon brown sugar
2 teaspoons fish sauce

1 Shell and devein shrimp, leaving tails intact. Combine prawns in medium bowl with sauce, oil, shrimp, chili, ginger and garlic. Refrigerate 30 minutes.

2 Meanwhile, place ingredients for lime dressing in screw-top jar; shake well.

3 Cook shrimp in large skillet over medium-high heat, in batches, until pink.

4 Combine shrimp, dressing and remaining ingredients in large bowl.

prep and cook time 35 minutes (+ refrigeration)   **serves** 4

shrimp & avocado salad

1½ pounds cooked medium shrimp
¼ pound sugar snap peas, trimmed
3 small avocados, thickly sliced
2 cups snow pea sprouts or watercress

chive vinaigrette
¼ cup white wine vinegar
¼ cup olive oil
¼ cup finely chopped fresh chives

1 Combine ingredients for chive vinaigrette in small bowl.

2 Shell shrimp if necessary, leaving tails intact.

3 Boil, steam or microwave peas until just tender; rinse under cold water, drain.

4 Place peas in large bowl with shrimp, avocado, sprouts and vinaigrette; toss gently to combine.

prep & cook time 25 minutes   **serves** 4

shrimp & mango salad

shrimp & avocado salad

turkey, fig & spinach salad

6 large fresh figs, quartered
4 cups baby spinach leaves
¼ pound salt and pepper shaved turkey breast,
  coarsely chopped

raspberry dressing
2 tablespoons raspberry vinegar
2 teaspoons walnut oil

1 Place ingredients for raspberry dressing in screw-top jar; shake well.

2 Place figs, spinach, turkey and dressing in large bowl; toss gently to combine. Season to taste with salt and pepper.

prep & cook time 10 minutes **serves** 4

chicken & cucumber salad

1 boneless, skinless chicken breast (about 6 ounces), thinly sliced
1 clove garlic, crushed
1 tablespoon lemon juice
1 teaspoon finely chopped fresh oregano
¼ teaspoon sweet paprika
2 slices lavash bread
1 teaspoon olive oil

cucumber salad
1 English cucumber, halved lengthways, thinly sliced
1 large green bell pepper, thinly sliced
4 roma tomatoes, seeded, thinly sliced
1 tablespoon coarsely chopped fresh dill
1 tablespoon coarsely chopped fresh oregano
¼ cup white wine vinegar
2 teaspoons sugar

1 Combine chicken, garlic, juice, oregano and paprika in medium bowl. Cover; refrigerate 30 minutes.

2 Meanwhile, preheat broiler. Arrange bread on a baking sheet; broil 1-2 minutes per side until lightly browned. Break bread into large pieces.

3 Make cucumber salad.

4 Warm oil in skillet over medium-high heat; cook chicken until cooked through.

5 Add chicken and bread to cucumber salad; toss gently. Serve immediately.

cucumber salad Combine ingredients in large bowl.

prep & cook time 25 minutes (+ refrigeration)
serves 4

tamarind honey chicken with Chinese cabbage salad

¼ cup peanut oil
¼ cup tamarind concentrate
1 tablespoon honey
2 teaspoons dark soy sauce
½ teaspoon fresh lime zest
1 tablespoon lime juice
1 clove garlic, crushed
4 boneless skinless chicken breast
   (about 6 ounces each)
½ small Chinese cabbage (¾ pound), trimmed,
   finely shredded
4 scallions, sliced thinly
1 pound red radishes, trimmed, thinly sliced,
   cut into matchsticks
2 cucumbers, halved widthways, seeded,
   cut into matchsticks
½ cup loosely packed fresh mint
½ cup loosely packed fresh cilantro
⅔ cup fried shallots

honey lime dressing
1 tablespoon honey
2 tablespoons lime juice
1 teaspoon sesame oil
1 tablespoon dark soy sauce
1 fresh long red chili, chopped finely

1 Combine 1 tablespoon of the oil, tamarind, honey, sauce, zest, juice, garlic and chicken in large bowl, cover; refrigerate 3 hours or overnight.

2 Place ingredients for honey lime dressing in screw-top jar; shake well.

3 Heat remaining oil in large skillet; cook chicken mixture, in batches, until cooked through. Stand 5 minutes; slice chicken thickly. Cover to keep warm.

4 Meanwhile, place dressing in large bowl with remaining ingredients; toss gently to combine.

5 Divide salad among plates; top with chicken.

prep & cook time 55 minutes (+ refrigeration)   **serves** 4

smoked chicken & peach salad

½ pound asparagus, trimmed, cut into 1½ lengths
1 cup pecans
1 pound smoked chicken breast, thinly sliced
1 small red onion, thinly sliced
2 peaches, thinly sliced
5 ounces baby spinach

dill vinaigrette
⅓ cup olive oil
2 tablespoons cider vinegar
1 tablespoon finely chopped fresh dill

1 Boil, steam or microwave asparagus until tender; drain. Rinse under cold water; drain.

2 Toast pecans in a dry skillet over medium-high heat until fragrant.

3 Place ingredients for dill vinaigrette in screw-top jar; shake well.

4 Place asparagus and vinaigrette with remaining ingredients in large bowl; toss gently to combine.

prep & cook time 20 minutes **serves** 4

smoked chicken & spinach salad

½ cup slivered almonds
¾ pound smoked chicken breast, thinly sliced
3 celery stalks, thinly sliced
3 small tomatoes, quartered, seeded
4 cups baby spinach
4 hard-boiled eggs, quartered
2 scallions, thinly sliced

cumin mayonnaise
½ cup mayonnaise
¼ cup lemon juice
½ teaspoon ground cumin

1 Make cumin mayonnaise.

2 Toast almonds in a dry skillet over medium-high heat until fragrant.

3 Place chicken, celery, tomato, spinach, egg, onion and nuts in large bowl; toss gently to combine.

4 Divide salad among serving plates; drizzle with mayonnaise.

cumin mayonnaise Combine mayonnaise, juice and cumin in small bowl.

prep & cook time 30 minutes **serves** 4

smoked chicken & peach salad

smoked chicken & spinach salad

tandoori chicken & spinach salad

⅓ cup tandoori paste
¼ cup plain yogurt
1½ pound chicken tenderloins
1 tablespoon vegetable oil
5 ounces baby spinach
2 cucumbers, thickly sliced
1 pint cherry tomatoes, halved
1 cup firmly packed fresh mint

spiced yogurt
1 clove garlic, crushed
¾ cup plain yogurt
1 tablespoon lemon juice
1 teaspoon ground cumin
1 teaspoon ground coriander

1 Combine paste and yogurt in medium bowl with chicken. Cover; refrigerate 3 hours or overnight.

2 Combine ingredients for spiced yogurt in small bowl.

3 Heat oil in large skillet; cook chicken mixture, in batches, until cooked through.

4 Place chicken in large bowl with spinach, cucumber, tomato and mint; toss gently to combine. Drizzle with yogurt.

prep & cook time 35 minutes (+ refrigeration) **serves** 4

chermoulla chicken salad

1 cup dried chickpeas
4 chicken breasts boneless, skinless (about 6 ounces each)
1 red bell pepper, finely chopped
1 green bell pepper, finely chopped
2 large roma tomatoes, finely chopped
1 small white onion, finely chopped
2 tablespoons lemon juice

chermoulla
½ cup finely chopped fresh cilantro
½ cup finely chopped fresh flat-leaf parsley
3 cloves garlic, crushed
2 tablespoons white wine vinegar
2 tablespoons lemon juice
1 teaspoon sweet paprika
½ teaspoon ground cumin
2 tablespoons olive oil

1 Place chickpeas in large bowl of cold water; stand overnight, drain. Rinse under cold water; drain. Cook chickpeas in medium saucepan of boiling water, uncovered, until just tender; drain. Rinse under cold water; drain.

2 Meanwhile, combine ingredients for chermoulla in large bowl; reserve half of the chermoulla for chickpea salad.

3 Place chicken in bowl with remaining half of the chermoulla; turn chicken to coat in chermoulla. Place a lightly oiled grill plate over medium-high heat. Cook chicken, in batches, until cooked through. Let stand 5 minutes; sliced chicken into thick pieces. Cover to keep warm.

4 Place chickpeas in large bowl with bell pepper, tomato, onion and remaining chermoulla; toss gently to combine. Serve salad with sliced chicken, drizzled with juice.

prep & cook time 40 minutes (+ standing) **serves** 4

tandoori chicken & spinach salad

chermoulla chicken salad

vietnamese chicken salad

1 pound boneless skinless chicken breasts
1 large carrot
½ cup rice wine vinegar
2 teaspoons salt
2 tablespoons sugar
1 white onion, thinly sliced
1½ cups bean sprouts
2 cups finely shredded savoy cabbage
¼ cup firmly packed fresh mint
½ cup firmly packed fresh cilantro
1 tablespoon crushed roasted peanuts
2 tablespoons fried shallots

Vietnamese dressing

2 tablespoons fish sauce
¼ cup water
2 tablespoons sugar
2 tablespoons lime juice
1 clove garlic, crushed

1 Place chicken in medium saucepan of gently boiling water; return to the boil. Reduce heat; simmer, uncovered, about 10 minutes or until cooked through. Cool chicken in poaching liquid 10 minutes; discard liquid (or reserve for another use). Shred chicken coarsely.

2 Meanwhile, cut carrot into matchstick-sized pieces. Combine carrot, vinegar, salt and sugar in large bowl, cover; stand 5 minutes. Add onion, cover; stand 5 minutes. Add sprouts, cover; stand 3 minutes. Drain pickled vegetables; discard liquid.

3 Place ingredients for Vietnamese dressing in screw-top jar; shake well.

4 Place pickled vegetables in large bowl with chicken, cabbage, mint, cilantro and dressing; toss gently to combine. Sprinkle with nuts and shallots.

prep & cook time 35 minutes   **serves** 4

chicken caesar salad

4 slices white bread
2 tablespoons olive oil
½ pound sliced bacon
3 cups coarsely chopped cooked chicken
1 large head romaine lettuce, trimmed, torn
6 scallions, thinly sliced
1 cup grated Parmesan cheese

caesar dressing
¾ cup mayonnaise
4 drained anchovy filets, finely chopped
1 tablespoon lemon juice
1 tablespoon Dijon mustard
1 tablespoon water

1 Preheat oven to 350°F (325°F convection).

2 Make caesar dressing.

3 Remove crusts from bread; discard crusts, cut bread into 1-inch squares; toss with oil in medium bowl. Place bread, in single layer, on baking sheet; toast in oven, 10 minutes.

4 Cook bacon in a skillet over medium heat, until browned and crisp. Drain on paper towels. Crumble when cool.

5 Combine half of the chicken, half of the bacon, half of the croutons and half of the dressing in large bowl with lettuce, half of the onion and half of the cheese; toss to combine.

6 Divide salad among serving plates. Top with remaining chicken, bacon, croutons, onion and cheese; drizzle with remaining dressing.

caesar dressing Blend or process ingredients until mixture is smooth.

prep & cook time 25 minutes **serves** 4

crispy duck & fig salad

4 boneless duck breasts (about 5 ounces each), skin on
4 cups watercress
1 pint yellow grape tomatoes, halved
4 fresh figs, cut into wedges

spiced balsamic glaze
½ cup balsamic vinegar
2 tablespoons brown sugar
½ teaspoon ground cinnamon
¼ teaspoon ground clove

1 Make spiced balsamic glaze.

2 Meanwhile, cook duck, skin-side down, in heated oiled skillet over medium heat about 5 minutes or until skin is crisp. Turn duck; cook about 5 minutes or until cooked as desired. Cover, stand 5 minutes, then slice duck thinly.

3 Place watercress and tomatoes in medium bowl with dressing; toss gently to combine. Divide figs among plates; top with tomato mixture then duck.

spiced balsamic glaze Stir ingredients in small saucepan over low heat, without boiling, until sugar dissolves. Bring to the boil; reduce heat. Simmer, uncovered, about 5 minutes or until syrup thickens slightly. Cool. If glaze becomes too thick, stir in a little boiling water.

prep & cook time 25 minutes **serves** 4

five-spice duck & peach salad

¼ cup honey
1 teaspoon five-spice powder
4 peaches, quartered
¼ pound snow peas, trimmed, halved on the diagonal
4 boneless duck breasts (about 5 ounces each), skin on
1 tablespoon red wine vinegar
2 tablespoons olive oil
1 teaspoon Dijon mustard
1 shallot, finely chopped
4 cups baby spinach

1 Cook honey, five-spice and peaches in large heated skillet, stirring, about 5 minutes or until peaches are lightly browned. Remove from pan; cover to keep warm.

2 Meanwhile, boil, steam or microwave snow peas until just tender; drain. Rinse under cold water; drain.

3 Score duck skins; cook duck, skin-side down, in same skillet, over medium heat, about 10 minutes or until browned and crisp. Turn duck; cook about 5 minutes or until cooked as desired. Remove from pan; cover to keep warm.

4 Combine vinegar, oil, mustard and shallot in large bowl. Add snow peas and spinach; toss gently to combine.

5 Slice duck thinly; serve with peaches and salad.

prep & cook time 30 minutes   **serves** 4

spicy pork & apple salad

¾ pound pork tenderloin
2 tablespoons lime juice
1 tablespoon finely chopped fresh oregano
2 cloves garlic, crushed
1 teaspoon ground cumin
2 teaspoons olive oil
6 cups watercress
2 apples, thickly sliced
1 pint red grape tomatoes, halved
2 tablespoons finely chopped fresh mint

1 Combine pork, juice, oregano, garlic and cumin in medium bowl.

2 Warm oil in a skillet over medium-high heat; cook pork until browned all over and cooked through. Cover; stand 10 minutes then slice pork thinly.

3 Place pork in large bowl with watercress, apple, tomatoes and mint. Serve with lime wedges, if desired.

prep & cook time 15 minutes   **serves** 4

pork & apple salad

1 pound pork tenderloin
2 tablespoons brown sugar
2 teaspoons wholegrain mustard
2 teaspoons fresh orange zest
1 tablespoon olive oil
1 tablespoon butter
1 green-skinned apple, unpeeled, halved, sliced
4 cups baby spinach

spiced orange dressing
¼ cup olive oil
2 tablespoons orange juice
1 tablespoon cider vinegar
½ teaspoon ground allspice

1 Combine pork, sugar, mustard and zest in medium bowl.

2 Heat oil in medium skillet; cook pork until cooked through. Cover pork; stand 5 minutes then slice thinly.

3 Melt butter in same skillet; cook apple until caramelised.

4 Meanwhile, place ingredients for spiced orange dressing in screw-top jar; shake well.

5 Place apple mixture, dressing and spinach in medium bowl; toss gently to combine. Arrange pork among serving plates; top with apple salad. Drizzle with any remaining dressing from bowl.

prep & cook time 30 minutes   **serves** 4

pancetta & mushroom salad

½ pound brown mushrooms, quartered
¼ cup balsamic vinegar
¼ pound pancetta
5 ounces baby spinach
2 tablespoons drained capers, rinsed
2 scallions, finely chopped
1 tablespoon olive oil
1 clove garlic, crushed

1 Combine mushrooms with 2 tablespoons of the vinegar in small bowl.

2 Cook pancetta in skillet over medium heat until crisp; chop coarsely.

3 Drain mushrooms; discard vinegar. Cook mushrooms in same skillet until tender.

4 Place pancetta, mushrooms and remaining vinegar in large large bowl with remaining ingredients; toss gently to combine.

prep & cook time 20 minutes   **serves** 6

pork & apple salad

pancetta & mushroom salad

gremolata lamb salad

- 8 ounces farfalle pasta
- 1 pound asparagus, trimmed, halved crossways
- ½ pound green beans, trimmed, halved crossways
- ⅓ cup pine nuts
- ⅓ cup loosely packed fresh flat-leaf parsley
- 1 tablespoon vegetable oil
- 1½ poundlamb loin
- 2 teaspoons Dijon mustard
- 3 shallots, thinly sliced

lemon Dijon dressing
- 2 tablespoons lemon juice
- 2 tablespoons extra virgin olive oil
- 2 teaspoons Dijon mustard

gremolata
- 2 cloves garlic, chopped finely
- 1 tablespoon fresh lemon zest
- ½ cup finely chopped fresh flat-leaf parsley

1 Make lemon Dijon dressing and gremolata.

2 Cook pasta in pot of boiling water, until just tender; drain. Rinse under cold water; drain.

3 Meanwhile, boil, steam or microwave asparagus and beans, separately, until just tender; drain.

4 Toast pine nuts in a dry skillet over medium-high heat until fragrant.

5 Heat oil in large skillet; cook lamb, uncovered, until browned and cooked as desired. Spread lamb with mustard; press gremolata firmly onto mustard on lamb. Cover; stand 5 minutes. Slice lamb thickly.

6 Place pasta, asparagus, beans and lamb in large bowl with shallots, pine nuts, parsley and dressing; toss gently to combine.

lemon Dijon dressing Place ingredients in screw-top jar; shake well.

gremolata Combine ingredients in small bowl.

prep & cook time 40 minutes **serves** 4

ratatouille & lamb salad

- 5 baby eggplants, thickly sliced
- 2 zucchini, thickly sliced
- 1 red onion, halved, cut into wedges
- 1 large red bell pepper, cut into 1-inch pieces
- 1 large yellow bell pepper, cut into 1-inch pieces
- 1 pint grape tomatoes
- 2 cloves garlic, crushed
- 3 tablespoons olive oil
- 1½ pound lamb loin
- 1 cup loosely packed fresh basil leaves
- 5 ounces firm goat cheese, crumbled

pesto dressing
- 1 tablespoon pine nuts
- 2 cloves garlic, crushed
- 2 tablespoons grated Parmesan cheese
- 1 tablespoon lemon juice
- ½ cup firmly packed fresh basil
- ½ cup olive oil

1 Preheat oven to 475°F (450°F convection). Oil two large shallow baking dishes.

2 Divide combined eggplant, zucchini, onion, bell pepper, tomatoes, garlic and 2 tablespoons oil between dishes. Roast, uncovered, about 20 minutes or until tender, stirring occasionally.

3 Meanwhile, make pesto dressing.

4 Heat remaining oil in large skiller; Cook lamb until browned and cooked as desired. Cover; stand 5 minutes. Slice lamb thickly.

5 Place vegetables in large bowl with basil and cheese; toss gently to combine. Divide vegetables among serving plates; top with lamb, drizzle with dressing.

pesto dressing Blend or process ingredients until smooth.

prep & cook time 55 minutes **serves** 4

gremolata lamb salad

ratatouille & lamb salad

vietnamese beef salad

¾ pound beef sirloin, thinly sliced
2 teaspoons fresh lime zest
¼ cup lime juice
1 tablespoon fish sauce
1 tablespoon brown sugar
1 clove garlic, crushed
1 stick (about 4 inches) lemon grass, crushed, finely chopped
1 fresh small red chili, finely chopped
1 piece (1 inch) fresh ginger, grated
¼ cup peanut oil
1 cup bean sprouts
1 red bell pepper, thinly sliced
1 carrot, cut into matchsticks
1 cup loosely packed vietnamese mint
1 cup loosely packed fresh cilantro

1 Combine beef, zest, juice, sauce, sugar, garlic, lemon grass, chili, ginger and 2 tablespoons of the oil in medium bowl; refrigerate 1 hour.

2 Heat remaining oil in wok; stir-fry beef mixture, in batches, until browned.

3 Place beef in large bowl with remaining ingredients; toss gently to combine.

prep & cook time 25 minutes (+ refrigeration) **serves** 4

beef & beets with horseradish crème fraîche

1 pound beef tenderloin, trimmed
2 tablespoons wholegrain mustard
1 tablespoon prepared horseradish
2 tablespoons olive oil
2 pounds baby beets, trimmed
5 ounces baby arugula
2 cucumbers, thinly sliced
1 cup loosely packed fresh flat-leaf parsley

parmesan croûtons
1 small loaf french bread
1 tablespoon olive oil
½ cup grated Parmesan cheese

horseradish crème fraîche
¼ cup crème fraîche
1 tablespoons prepared horseradish
1 tablespoon lemon juice

1 Preheat oven to 450°F (425°F convection).

2 Tie beef with kitchen string at 1½ inch intervals. Combine mustard, horseradish and oil in small bowl; brush beef all over with mixture.

3 Place beef in medium oiled baking dish with beets; roast, uncovered, 10 minutes.

4 Reduce heat to 400°F (375°F convection); roast about 20 minutes or until beef and beets are cooked. Cover beef; stand 15 minutes then slice thinly. Peel and halve beets.

5 Make Parmesan croutons and horseradish crème fraîche.

6 Place arugula, cucumber, parsley and beets in large bowl; toss gently to combine. Serve salad topped with croutons and beef, drizzled with crème fraîche.

parmesan croûtons Slice bread thinly; brush slices with oil, place on baking sheet. Brown, in oven, towards end of beef cooking time; sprinkle with cheese, return to oven until cheese melts.

horseradish crème fraîche Combine ingredients in small bowl.

prep & cook time 45 minutes (+ standing) **serves** 4

chorizo & roasted pepper salad

2 large red bell peppers
2 chorizo sausages (about 6 ounces each), thinly sliced
1 can (14 ounces) artichoke hearts, drained, halved
½ pint red grape tomatoes, halved
4 cups curly endive
½ cup firmly packed fresh flat-leaf parsley

herb and garlic dressing
2 tablespoons olive oil
2 tablespoons white wine vinegar
1 tablespoon lemon juice
1 tablespoon finely chopped fresh basil
1 tablespoon finely chopped fresh oregano
2 cloves garlic, finely chopped

1 Preheat broiler. Quarter bell peppers; discard seeds and membranes; arrange on a baking sheet, skin-side up. Broil until skin blisters and blackens. Place peppers in a covered bowl and let stand for 5 minutes; peel away skin then cut pieces in half diagonally.

2 Meanwhile, cook chorizo in large skillet over medium-high heat, stirring occasionally, until browned. Drain on paper towels.

3 Combine ingredients for herb and garlic dressing in small bowl.

4 Place bell peppers, chorizo and dressing in large bowl with remaining ingredients; toss gently to combine.

prep & cook time 25 minutes **serves** 4

cajun-spiced beef salad

1½ pounds piece beef sirloin
1 tablespoon Cajun spice mix
½ can (15 ounces) cannellini beans, rinsed, drained
2 cucumbers, halved lengthways, thinly sliced
4 small tomatoes, cut into wedges
1 red onion, thinly sliced
1 avocado, thickly sliced
½ cup finely chopped fresh cilantro

garlic vinaigrette
¼ cup lemon juice
¼ cup olive oil
2 cloves garlic, crushed

1 Combine ingredients for garlic vinaigrette in small bowl.

2 Sprinkle beef both sides with spice mix. Place an oiled grill plate over medium-high heat; cook beef to desired doneness. Cover; stand 5 minutes then slice thinly.

3 Place remaining ingredients in large bowl with dressing; toss gently to combine.

4 Serve salad topped with beef.

prep & cook time 25 minutes **serves** 4

chorizo & roasted pepper salad

cajun-spiced beef salad

beet & lentil salad
with grilled sausages

1½ cups small brown lentils
2 sprigs fresh thyme
1½ small beets, trimmed
1 tablespoon olive oil
1 large onion, finely chopped
2 teaspoons mustard seed
2 teaspoons ground cumin
1 teaspoon ground coriander
½ cup chicken stock
5 ounces baby spinach
8 thick pork sausages (about 4 ounces each)

thyme dressing
1 teaspoon fresh thyme
1 clove garlic, crushed
½ cup red wine vinegar
¼ cup olive oil

1 Place ingredients for thyme dressing in screw-top jar; shake well.

2 Cook lentils and thyme, uncovered, in large pot of boiling water until lentils are just tender; drain, discard thyme. Place lentils in large bowl with half of the dressing; toss gently to combine.

3 Meanwhile, discard any leaves and all but 1-inch of the stalk from each beet. Boil, steam or microwave unpeeled beets until just tender; drain. When cool enough to handle, peel then quarter each beet; place in bowl with lentils.

4 Heat oil in large skillet; cook onion, seeds and spices, stirring, until onion softens. Add stock; bring to the boil. Remove from heat; stir in spinach.

5 Place spinach mixture and remaining dressing in bowl with beet and lentil mixture; toss gently to combine.

6 Cook sausages in same cleaned skillet until cooked through; serve sliced sausages with beet and lentil salad.

prep & cook time 1 hour **serves** 4

fruit salads

roasted pear & spinach salad

4 medium pears, peeled, cored, sliced thickly
2 tablespoons lemon juice
2 tablespoons brown sugar
5 ounces baby spinach leaves
1 cup baby arugula leaves
¼ cup flaked parmesan cheese
¼ cup coarsely chopped fresh chives

balsamic mustard dressing
2 tablespoons balsamic vinegar
1 tablespoon wholegrain mustard
1 teaspoon olive oil

1 Preheat oven to 400°F (375°F convection). Line baking sheet with parchment paper.

2 Combine pears, juice and sugar in large bowl. Place pears, in single layer, on baking sheet; roast, uncovered, about 30 minutes, brushing with juices occasionally, or until tender. Cool 20 minutes.

3 Meanwhile, place ingredients for balsamic mustard dressing in screw-top jar; shake well.

4 Place pears and dressing in large bowl with spinach, arugula, cheese and chives; toss gently to combine.

prep & cook time 40 minutes (+ cooling) **serves** 4

orange & radish salad

10 trimmed red radishes, thinly sliced
4 large oranges, segmented
1 small red onion, thinly sliced
2 tablespoons coarsely chopped fresh flat-leaf parsley
2 tablespoons coarsely chopped fresh cilantro
¼ cup orange juice

1 Assemble radish, orange and onion on serving platter; sprinkle with parsley and cilantro, drizzle with juice.

2 Cover salad; refrigerate 1 hour before serving.

prep time 20 minutes (+ refrigeration) **serves** 4

roasted pear & spinach salad

orange & radish salad

balsamic strawberries

1 pound strawberries, halved
2 tablespoons confectioners' sugar
1 tablespoon balsamic vinegar
¼ cup loosely packed fresh mint
½ cup plain yogurt

1 Combine strawberries, sugar and vinegar in medium bowl. Cover; refrigerate 20 minutes.

2 Sprinkle mint over strawberries; serve with yogurt.

prep time 10 minutes (+ refrigeration) **serves** 4

strawberries in orange syrup

¼ cup water
2 tablespoons brown sugar
2 teaspoons fresh orange zest
2 tablespoons orange juice
1 pound strawberries, quartered
¼ cup coarsely chopped fresh mint
⅔ cup crème fraîche

1 Stir sugar in small saucepan, over low heat, until sugar dissolves; bring to the boil. Boil, uncovered, without stirring, about 3 minutes or until syrup thickens slightly. Remove from heat; stir in rind and juice. Cool.

2 Combine strawberries and in medium bowl with syrup; refrigerate 30 minutes.

3 Divide strawberry mixture among bowls; serve with crème fraîche.

prep & cook time 20 minutes (+ cooling & refrigeration) **serves** 4

balsamic strawberries

strawberries in orange syrup

summer fruit salad with minted sugar

¼ cup loosely packed fresh mint
2 tablespoons sugar
2 teaspoons fresh lemon zest
2 pears, cored, sliced thinly
1 cup blackberries
2 cups strawberries, halved
1 cup seedless green grapes, halved

1 Blend or process mint, sugar and zest until chopped finely.

2 Combine fruit in medium bowl. Serve fruit salad with minted sugar.

prep time 15 minutes **serves** 4

strawberries romanoff

1 pound strawberries, halved
1½ tablespoons orange-flavored liqueur
2 teaspoons confectioners' sugar
2 tablespoons confectioners' sugar, extra
½ cup heavy whipping cream

1 Combine strawberries, liqueur and sugar in large bowl; refrigerate 30 minutes. Drain strawberries over small bowl; reserve liquid. Divide three-quarters of the strawberries among serving dishes.

2 Blend or process remaining strawberries, extra 2 tablespoons sugar and reserved liquid until smooth. Beat cream in small bowl with electric mixer until soft peaks form; fold in strawberry mixture.

3 Top strawberries with strawberry cream.

prep time 15 minutes (+ refrigeration) **serves** 4

summer fruit salad with minted sugar

strawberries romanoff

watermelon, mint & feta salad

2 teaspoons sugar
¼ cup lime juice
½ cup crumbled feta cheese
½ small red onion, thinly sliced
½ cup coarsely chopped fresh mint
1½ pound seedless watermelon, cut into wedges

1 Dissolve sugar in bowl with juice.

2 Combine juice mixture with cheese, onion and mint.

3 Arrange watermelon on serving plates; spoon cheese mixture over watermelon.

prep time 10 minutes   **serves** 4

watermelon & berry salad

1 piece seedless watermelon (about 4 pounds)
½ pound strawberries, halved
¼ pound blueberries
¼ cup loosely packed fresh mint

1 Using melon baller, cut watermelon balls.

2 Combine watermelon in medium bowl with berries and mint.

prep time 10 minutes **serves** 4

watermelon with chili herbed salad

2 limes
½ seedless watermelon (about 6 pounds)
1 fresh long red chili, chopped finely
½ cup finely chopped fresh cilantro
¼ cup fresh mint
½ cup baby greens, such tat soi

lime dressing
¼ cup lime juice
¼ cup olive oil

1 Cut thin strips of zest from one lime then chop finely; reserve for lime dressing. Peel remaining lime; segment both limes then chop coarsely.

2 Remove and discard skin and white pith from watermelon; cut watermelon in half, then cut into eight 2" x 4" blocks. Cut blocks into six ½ inch slices.

3 Make lime dressing.

4 Place lime in medium bowl with chili, cilantro, mint and tat soi in; toss gently to combine.

5 Layer watermelon on large platter; sprinkle over lime and herb mixture, drizzle with dressing.

lime dressing Place juice, oil and reserved zest in screw-top jar; shake well.

prep time 15 minutes **serves** 8

tropical fruit with orange glaze

1 teaspoon finely grated orange rind
2 tablespoons orange juice
2 tablespoons brown sugar
1 small pineapple, trimmed, halved, sliced thickly
2 medium bananas, quartered
1 star fruit, sliced thickly
¼ cup loosely packed fresh mint leaves

1 To make orange glaze, stir rind, juice and sugar in small saucepan over low heat until sugar dissolves. Cool.

2 Preheat grill.

3 Place glaze in large bowl with fruit; stir to combine. Spread fruit mixture onto two foil-lined oven trays.

4 Grill fruit about 5 minutes or until browned lightly. Serve fruit sprinkled with mint.

prep & cook time 20 minutes **serves** 4

salad dressings

arugula & garlic dressing

1 cup mayonnaise
1 cup baby arugula
1 clove garlic, crushed
1 teaspoon fresh lemon zest

1 Blend or process ingredients until smooth.

prep time 10 minutes   **makes** 1¼ cup

green goddess dressing

1 cup mayonnaise
2 drained anchovy filets, finely chopped
2 scallions, thinly sliced
2 teaspoons finely chopped fresh flat-leaf parsley
2 teaspoons finely chopped fresh chives
2 teaspoons finely chopped fresh tarragon
2 teaspoons cider vinegar

1 Combine ingredients in small bowl.

prep time 10 minutes   **makes** 1¼ cup

arugula & garlic dressing

green goddess dressing

ginger miso dressing

classic italian dressing

classic french dressing

red berry vinaigrette

ginger miso dressing

¼ cup rice vinegar
2 tablespoons white miso
1 tablespoon mirin
2 teaspoons sugar
1 piece (about 1 inch) fresh ginger, grated
1 clove garlic, crushed
1 teaspoon soy sauce
1 teaspoon sesame oil
1 tablespoon water

1 Stir ingredients in small saucepan, over low heat, until sugar dissolves.

2 Remove pan from heat, strain over small jug; discard solids.

prep & cook time 20 minutes **makes** ½ cup

classic french dressing

¼ cup white vinegar
¾ cup olive oil
½ teaspoon sugar
1 teaspoon Dijon mustard

1 Place ingredients in screw-top jar; shake well.

prep time 10 minutes **makes** about 1 cup

classic italian dressing

2 tablespoons white wine vinegar
2 tablespoons lemon juice
½ teaspoon sugar
2 cloves garlic, crushed
¾ cup olive oil
1 tablespoon finely chopped fresh basil
1 tablespoon finely chopped fresh oregano

1 Place ingredients in screw-top jar; shake well.

prep time 10 minutes **makes** about 1 cup

red berry vinaigrette

¼ cup red wine vinegar
½ cup olive oil
½ cup fresh raspberries
¼ cup whole berry cranberry sauce

1 Blend or process ingredients until smooth.

2 Push dressing through fine sieve into small bowl.

prep time 5 minutes **makes** 1 cup

Use raspberry or pomegranate vinegar in place of red wine vinegar for an extra fruity taste. If dressing is too thick, stir in a little cold water until dressing is desired consistency.

oregano & caper dressing

2 hard-boiled eggs, quartered
1 tablespoon drained capers, rinsed
2 tablespoons white wine vinegar
2 tablespoons coarsely chopped fresh oregano
1 clove garlic, quartered
⅓ cup olive oil

1 Blend or process egg, capers, vinegar, oregano and garlic until smooth.

2 With motor operating, add oil in a thin, steady stream; blend until dressing thickens.

prep time 10 minutes   **makes** 1 cup

rosemary balsamic dressing

2 tablespoons olive oil
1 tablespoon balsamic vinegar
1 tablespoon lemon juice
1 tablespoon coarsely chopped fresh rosemary

1 Place ingredients in screw-top jar; shake well.

prep time 10 minutes   **makes** ⅓ cup

ranch dressing

½ cup mayonnaise
¼ cup buttermilk
1 tablespoon white wine vinegar
½ small onion, chopped finely
1 clove garlic, crushed
1 tablespoon finely chopped fresh chives
1 tablespoon finely chopped fresh flat-leaf parsley
¼ teaspoon sweet paprika

1 Whisk ingredients in small bowl until combined.

prep time 10 minutes   **makes** 1 cup

classic mayonnaise

2 egg yolks
½ teaspoon salt
1 teaspoon Dijon mustard
⅔ cup extra light olive oil
⅓ cup olive oil
1 tablespoon white wine vinegar
1 tablespoon lemon juice

1 Combine egg yolks, salt and mustard in medium bowl. Gradually add oils in a thin, steady stream, whisking constantly until mixture thickens. Stir in vinegar and juice.

prep time 15 minutes   **makes** 1 cup

oregano & caper dressing

ranch dressing

rosemary balsamic dressing

classic mayonnaise

lemon & chive vinaigrette

2 cloves garlic, crushed
¼ cup white wine vinegar
1 tablespoon fresh lemon zest
½ cup olive oil
1 tablespoon coarsely chopped fresh chives

1 Place garlic, vinegar, zest and oil in screw-top jar; shake well. Add chives.

prep time 10 minutes   **makes** ¾ cup

classic russian dressing

1 large beet, trimmed
2 tablespoons coarsely chopped pickled onions
1 tablespoon drained capers, rinsed
½ cup sour cream

1 Boil, steam or microwave beet until tender; drain, reserving ¼ cup of the cooking liquid. When cool enough to handle, peel then chop beet coarsely.

2 Blend or process beet with remaining ingredients and reserved liquid until smooth.

prep & cook time 35 minutes   **makes** 1½ cup

A small can of beets, drained and chopped, can be used instead of fresh beetroot.

orange & chili vinaigrette

1 cup orange juice
1 fresh long red chili, coarsely chopped
1 teaspoon fresh orange zest
2 teaspoons Dijon mustard
½ cup olive oil

1 Place juice in small saucepan; simmer, uncovered, about 10 minutes or until liquid reduces to a third of a cup. Add chili and zest; cool to room temperature.

2 Blend or process juice mixture with mustard until smooth. With motor operating, gradually add oil in thin, steady stream; process until dressing thickens.

prep & cook time 15 minutes (+ cooling)
makes 1 cup

classic pesto dressing

1 tablespoon pine nuts
2 cloves garlic, crushed
¼ cup grated Parmesan cheese
1 tablespoon lemon juice
1 cup firmly packed fresh basil
⅓ cup olive oil
½ cup buttermilk

1 Toast pine nuts in a skillet over medium-high heat until fragrant.

2 Blend or process nuts, garlic, cheese, juice, basil and oil until smooth.

3 Transfer basil mixture to small bowl; stir in buttermilk.

prep time 10 minutes   **makes** 1 cup

lemon & chive vinaigrette

orange & chili vinaigrette

classic russian dressing

classic pesto dressing

glossary

Allspice also known as pimento or jamaican pepper; so-named because it tastes like a combination of nutmeg, cumin, clove and cinnamon. Available whole or ground.

Artichoke heart tender center of the globe artichoke; harvested from the plant after the prickly choke is removed. Buy from delicatessens or canned in brine.

Beans
cannellini small white bean similar in appearance and flavor to other phaseolus vulgaris varieties (great northern, navy or haricot). Available dried or canned.
fava also known as broad beans; available dried, fresh, canned and frozen. Fresh and frozen forms should be peeled twice (discarding both the outer long green pod and the beige-green tough inner shell).
green also known as French or string beans; this long thin fresh bean is consumed in its entirety once cooked.
kidney medium-sized red bean, slightly floury in texture yet sweet in flavor; sold dried or canned.
lima large, flat kidney-shaped, beige dried and canned beans. Also known as butter beans.
sprouts tender new shoots of assorted beans and seeds germinated for consumption as sprouts (including mung beans, soy beans, alfalfa and snow pea sprouts).
white in this book, some recipes may simply call for ''white beans,'' a generic term used for canned or dried cannellini, navy or great northern beans.

Bell peppers come in many colors: red, green, yellow, orange and purplish-black. Discard seeds and membranes before use.

Breads
ciabatta in Italian, the word means slipper, which is the traditional shape of this popular white bread with a crisp crust.
flat breads also known as roti, or chapatti. Made of wheat and water and used for scooping or wrapping.
focaccia a popular Italian flat, yeast bread. The top is dimpled and brushed with oil to keep the bread moist and flavorful. The most basic focaccia is simply a herbed and oiled bread with salt, but the variations are endless.
french a long, narrow cylindrical loaf with a crisp brown crust and light chewy interior. A standard loaf is 4-5'' wide and 1-2'' tall, but can be up to 2 feet in length.
lavash flat, unleavened bread of Mediterranean origin.
pita also known as lebanese bread. This wheat-flour pocket bread is sold in large, flat pieces that separate into two thin rounds. Also available in small pieces called pocket pita.
sourdough so-named, not because it's sour in taste, but because it's made by using a small amount of ''starter dough,'' which contains a yeast culture, mixed into flour and water. Part of the resulting dough is then saved to use as the starter dough next time.
tortilla thin, round, unleavened bread originating in Mexico. Two kinds are available, one made from wheat flour and the other from corn.

Broccolini a cross between broccoli and Chinese kale; has long asparagus-like stems with a long loose floret, both completely edible. Resembles broccoli in look but is milder and sweeter in taste.

Bulgur hulled steamed wheat kernels that, once dried, are crushed into various size grains. Not the same as cracked wheat. Found in health food stores or most supermarkets.

Butter use salted or unsalted (sweet) butter; 125g is equal to one stick (4 ounces) of butter.

Buttermilk originally the term given to the slightly sour liquid left after butter was churned from cream, today it is made similarly to yogurt. Found in the refrigerated section in supermarkets. Despite its name, it is low in fat.

Camembert cheese *see* Cheese

Caper berries fruit formed after the caper buds have flowered; caper berries are pickled, usually with their stalks intact.

Capers the grey-green buds of a warm climate shrub (usually Mediterranean); sold either dried and salted, or pickled in a vinegar brine. Baby capers are smaller, fuller-flavored and more expensive than the full-sized ones. Capers should be rinsed well before using.

Cheese
bocconcini from ''boccone'', meaning mouthful in Italian; a walnut-sized baby mozzarella. Is a delicate, semi-soft, white cheese. Sold fresh, it spoils rapidly so will only keep for one or two days refrigerated in brine.
brie often referred to in France as the queen of cheeses; soft-ripened cow-milk cheese with a delicate, creamy texture and a rich, sweet taste that varies from buttery to mushroomy.
cheddar the most common cows-milk cheese; should be aged, hard and have a pronounced bite.
cream commonly known as Philadelphia or Philly; a soft cows-milk cheese. Also available as spreadable light cream cheese.
feta a crumbly textured goat- or sheep-milk cheese having a sharp, salty taste. Ripened and stored in salted whey.
goat made from goat milk; has an earthy, strong taste. Available in soft, crumbly and firm textures, in various shapes and sizes, and sometimes rolled in ash or herbs.
haloumi has a semi-firm, spongy texture and very salty yet sweet flavor. Ripened and stored in salted whey, it holds its shape well when heated. Best eaten while still warm as it becomes rubbery when cool.
mozzarella soft, spun-curd cheese; most popular pizza cheese because of its low melting point and elasticity when heated.
parmesan also known as parmigiana; a hard, grainy cows-milk cheese.
ricotta a soft, white, sweet, cows-milk cheese having a slightly grainy texture. The name roughly translates as ''cooked again'' and refers to ricotta's manufacture from a whey that is itself a by-product of other cheese making.

Chickpeas also known as garbanzos; an irregularly round, sandy-colored legume.

Chilies always use rubber gloves when seeding and chopping fresh chilies as they can burn your skin. Unseeded chilies were used to develop these recipes because the seeds contain the heat; use fewer chilies rather than seeding the lot.

chipotle (cheh-pote-lay) the name used for jalapeño chilies once they've been dried and smoked. Has a deep, intensely smoky flavor, rather than a searing heat; are dark brown, almost black in color and wrinkled in appearance. Often sold canned in adobo sauce.

flakes also sold as crushed chili; dehydrated deep red extremely fine slices and whole seeds.

green any unripened chili; also some particular varieties that are ripe when green, such as jalapeño, habanero, poblano or serrano.

jalapeño fairly hot green chilies, available in brine, bottled, or fresh.

long red available both fresh and dried; a generic term used for any moderately hot, long, thin chili.

Coconut milk not the liquid found inside the fruit (called coconut water), but the diluted liquid from the second pressing of the white flesh of a mature coconut. Available in cans and cartons at most supermarkets.

Couscous a fine, grain-like cereal product made from semolina. A semolina flour and water dough is sieved then dehydrated to produce minuscule even-sized pellets of couscous; it is rehydrated by steaming, or with the addition of a warm liquid, and swells to three or four times its original size.

Crème fraîche a fermented cream with a tangy, nutty flavor and velvety texture.

Currants, dried tiny, almost black raisins so-named after a grape variety that originated in Corinth, Greece.

Curry powder a blend of ground spices used for making Indian and some South-East Asian dishes. Consists of some of the following spices: dried chilies, cinnamon, coriander, cumin, fennel, fenugreek, mace, cardamom and turmeric. Available mild or hot.

Fennel also known as finocchio or anise; a white to very pale green-white, firm, crisp, roundish vegetable. The bulb has a slightly sweet, anise flavor but the leaves have a much stronger taste. Also the name given to dried seeds having a licorice flavor.

Figs vary in skin and flesh color according to type, not ripeness. When ripe, should be unblemished and bursting with flesh; nectar beads at the base indicate when it's at its best.

Five-spice powder a fragrant mixture of cinnamon, cloves, star anise, sichuan pepper and fennel seeds. Also known as chinese five-spice.

Ginger
fresh also known as green or root ginger; the thick gnarled root of a tropical plant.
ground also called powdered ginger; used as a flavoring in baking but cannot be substituted for fresh ginger.
pickled pink or red colored; available, packaged, from Asian food shops. Pickled paper-thin shavings of ginger in a mixture of vinegar, sugar and natural coloring; used in Japanese cooking.

Leek a member of the onion family; looks like a large green onion but is more subtle and mild in flavor. Wash well before use. Pencil leeks, young, slender leeks, can be cooked and eaten like asparagus.

Olives
green harvested before fully ripened and are, as a rule, denser and more bitter than their black or brown relatives.
kalamata small, sharp-tasting brine-cured black olives.
niçoise small black olives.

Onions
fried sold in Asian grocery stores packed in jars or in cellophane bags. Make your own by cutting onions into paper-thin slices, then deep-frying in peanut oil; drain on absorbent paper before storing in an airtight container.
red also known as Spanish, red Spanish or bermuda onion; a sweet-flavored, large, purple-red onion.
scallion also known as green onions; an immature onion picked before the bulb has formed, having a long, bright-green edible stalk.
shallot also called french or golden shallot or eschalot; small, brown-skinned member of the onion family. Grows in tight clusters similar to garlic.
spring crisp, narrow green-leafed tops and a round sweet white bulb; larger than green onions.
yellow and white are interchangeable. Their pungent flesh adds flavor to a vast range of dishes.

Pancetta an Italian unsmoked bacon; pork belly that is cured

in salt and spices then rolled into a sausage shape and dried for several weeks.

Polenta also known as cornmeal; a flour-like cereal made of dried corn (maize); sold ground in different textures. Also the name of the dish made from it.

Pomegranate native to the Middle East; a dark-red, leathery-skinned fresh fruit about the size of a large orange. Each fruit is filled with hundreds of seeds, each wrapped in an edible crimson pulp having a unique tangy sweet-sour flavor.

Poppy seeds
black small, dried, bluish-grey seeds of the poppy plant, with a crunchy texture and a nutty flavor. Can be purchased whole or ground in most supermarkets.
white also known as kas kas. Quite dissimilar to the black variety, these seeds from the white poppy are used, ground, as a thickening agent in sauces or as a substitute for ground almonds.

Prosciutto cured, air-dried (unsmoked), pressed ham.

Sauces
barbecue a spicy, tomato-based sauce used to marinate or baste, or as a condiment.
dark soy deep brown, almost black in color; rich, with a thicker consistency than other types. Pungent but not particularly salty.
fish also called nam pla or nuoc nam; made from pulverized salted fermented fish, most often anchovies. Has a pungent smell and strong taste. There are many versions of varying intensity, so use according to your taste.

hoisin a thick, sweet and spicy Chinese paste made from salted fermented soy beans, onions and garlic. Used as a marinade or a baste, or to accent stir-fries.

oyster Asian in origin, this rich, brown sauce is made from oysters and their brine, cooked with salt and soy sauce, and thickened with starches.

soy made from fermented soy beans. There are several variations available. For these recipes use a mild Japanese variety unless otherwise indicated.

Worcestershire a spicy dark-colored sauce made from garlic, soy sauce, onions, lime, tamarind, molasses, anchovies, vinegar and seasonings. This condiment was invented by the English in India.

Squash, yellow patty-pan a round, slightly flat summer squash being yellow to pale-green in color and having a scalloped edge. Harvested young, it has a firm white flesh and a distinct flavor.

Star fruit also known as carambola, pale green or yellow in color, it has a clean, crisp texture. Flavor may be either sweet or sour, depending on the variety and when it was picked. There is no need to peel or seed it and they're slow to discolor.

Tahini a rich sesame-seed paste available from Middle-Eastern grocery stores and health-food shops; often used in hummus, baba ghanoush and other Lebanese recipes.

Tamarind concentrate the commercial distillation of tamarind pulp into a condensed paste. Thick and purple-black, it is ready-to-use, with no soaking or straining required; can be diluted with water according to taste. Found in Asian supermarkets.

Tomatoes
cherry also known as tom thumb tomatoes; small, round tomatoes.
grape small, long oval-shaped tomatoes with a good flavor.
roma also called plum or roma, these are smallish, oval-shaped tomatoes.
sun-dried in oil tomato pieces that have been dried with salt; this dehydrates the tomato and concentrates the flavor. Use sun-dried tomatoes packaged in oil for these recipes, unless otherwise specified.

Yogurt Use plain full-cream yogurt in these recipes unless specifically noted otherwise. If a recipe in this book calls for low-fat yogurt, use one with a fat content of less than 0.2 per cent.

index

STERLING

New York

An Imprint of Sterling Publishing
387 Park Avenue South
New York, NY 10016

ISBN 978-1-4549-1018-3

Distributed in Canada by Sterling Publishing
c/o Canadian Manda Group, 165 Dufferin Street
Toronto, Ontario, Canada M6K 3H6

For information about custom editions, special sales, and premium and corporate purchases,
please contact Sterling Special Sales at 800-805-5489 or specialsales@sterlingpublishing.com.

Manufactured in the China

2 4 6 8 10 9 7 5 3 1

www.sterlingpublishing.com